Pontius, the Pilot

Also by Richard Huggett

Pontius, the Pilot

The best of Catholic jokes, wit and humour

COMPILED BY RICHARD HUGGETT

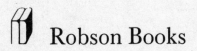 Robson Books

First published in Great Britain in hardback in 1986 by Robson Books Ltd, Bolsover House, 5–6 Clipstone Street, London W1P 7EB. This Robson paperback edition first published in 1987.

British Library Cataloguing in Publication Data

Pontius the pilot: the best of Catholic
    jokes, wit and humour.
    1. Catholic Church——Anecdotes, facetiae,
    satire, etc.   2. English wit and humour
    I. Huggett, Richard. 1929–
    828'.91407'080382   PN6231.C/

ISBN 0-86051-468-4

Typeset by Bookworm Typesetting, Manchester

Printed in Great Britain by
Biddles Ltd, Guildford and King's Lynn

Dedication

I wish to dedicate this book to Father Maurus Powell, O.S.B., the Headmaster of Gilling Castle which was, and happily still is, Ampleforth College's prep school, and I count myself highly privileged that for five glorious years I came under his influence and learned so much which was to be of value in later life. A strict disciplinarian, he was essentially a kindly, generous and lovable man, and it was from him during his Easter sermons that I heard many of these jokes – particularly that which gives this book its title.

Contents

Introduction

IT'S SAFE TO assume that 80 per cent of those in the theatre are either Catholics or Jews (with the exception of the late Ernest Milton who cleverly contrived to be both at one and the same time). So it seemed like a good idea to publish my appeal for Catholic jokes in *The Stage*. It was. I had a huge response of some hundreds. The trouble was that so many of them were the same, and I'm convinced that each person was convinced that theirs was the first and only time anybody had written it down and sent it to me.

After a few weeks I learned to dread the sight of a cheap envelope revealing a sheet of lined paper torn out of a school exercise book illegibly scrawled with little attention paid to spelling, grammar and punctuation and sent from some remote convent in Western Ireland. It invariably revealed the nun from Lourdes joke, the 'make me a novena' joke or the nun who wanted to be a prostitute.

But I mustn't be unkind. I'm grateful to the public's response, and all those people who have written have helped me in my search for what I have, perhaps immodestly, described as 'the best of Catholic jokes, wit and humour'.

It is the non-Catholics who are shocked by Catholic jokes, but we Catholics adore them and have always enjoyed telling and re-telling them. At Ampleforth we had some very witty priests, and my memories of the chapel at Gilling Castle is that we spent as much time laughing as praying. Laughter seems to me to be an entirely satisfactory way of getting to know the God who made us, even if we start having doubts in later life. But even doubts can be funny.

Richard Huggett, 1986

Doctrines and Dogmas

Godfrey Smith, *Sunday Times* columnist, once interviewed the 16th Duke of Norfolk.

'Have you ever had doubts about the validity of your church's doctrines and practices?'

'No, by Jove, I haven't,' barked the Duke. But after a long pause, he added, 'But if I'd had a little more intelligence, I might have done.'

*   *   *   *   *

Cardinal Cushing of Boston provided a telling illustration in an address at a meeting of Episcopalian priests. As a parish priest he was called to the side of a man who had collapsed on the floor of a department store. The then Father Cushing asked the man: 'Do you believe in God the Father, God the Son and God the Holy Ghost?'

The man opened one eye and said to those standing about: 'Here I am dying, and he's asking me riddles.'

*   *   *   *   *

A famous Catholic writer, whom we will call Patrick Smith, once attempted to explain to the late Victor Gollancz, Jewish publisher, the Church's teaching on the subject of death-bed repentance. 'If you make an act of perfect contrition before you die, then you will go to heaven eventually, no matter how sinful your life has been,' he said.

Gollancz was politely incredulous. 'Do you mean to tell me that if a man was committing what you call the mortal sin of fornication and died of a heart attack while he was enjoying his climax, all he needs to do to enjoy eternal bliss is to say he's sorry as long as he says it before the moment of death . . . . is this *really* what you Catholics teach?'

Smith nodded. 'Yes,' he said, 'but it must be a really perfect act of contrition, he must be sincerely sorry.'

'Supposing it wasn't perfect?' asked Gollancz, 'supposing he was only pretending to be sorry, would he then go to hell?'

'Yes, he probably would,' said Smith.

It was this conversation which inspired Gollancz to write the following limerick:

> While engaged in his final emission,
> Patrick Smith's soul flew off to perdition.
> It wasn't the ****
> Which caused this bad luck
> But an act of imperfect contrition.

*   *   *   *   *

Schoolboy definition of faith:
Believing in something you absolutely know isn't true.

*   *   *   *   *

The Church's law of not eating meat on Friday has, over the centuries, attracted a great deal of scorn. Here is Dean Swift on the subject:

> Does any man of commonsense
> Think ham and beef give God offence?
> Or that a herring has the charm
> The Almighty's anger to disarm?
> Wrapped up in His Majesty divine
> D'you think he cares on what we dine?

There was a young man who said 'Run,
The end of the world has begun.
It's that Holy Ghost
That I fear the most.
I'm friends with the Father and Son.'

*　　*　　*　　*　　*

I'd hoped
The Pope'd
Not Kill
The Pill.

*　　*　　*　　*　　*

Cardinal Manning
Abhorred family planning
Like Cardinal Newman
He thought it inhuman.

*　　*　　*　　*　　*

The teacher was instructing a class of boys about the Immaculate Conception, informing them that this was God's especial and unique gift of Grace to Mary's soul, the Virgin Birth being an added gift to her body. She asked: 'What is the difference between the Immaculate Conception and the Virgin Birth?' A swift answer came from a boy in the front row:
　'Nine months.'

*　　*　　*　　*　　*

An old lady in a remote part of Ireland said to her parish priest: 'Father, can you tell me what is the difference between Cherubim and Seraphim?'

The priest replied: 'Well now, I believe there was a wee difference between them once, but I hear they're the best of friends again now.'

* * * * *

A punter at the races noticed a priest making strange hand signs over a horse parading in the paddock. The horse won. Next race the same thing occurred, strange hand signs in the paddock and the horse won. The punter approached the priest and asked him what he was doing. 'I'm blessing him,' was the reply. Watching the priest closely when he did the same thing for the third race, the punter rushed to put all his money on the same horse, but the horse collapsed in the middle of the race and died.

Crestfallen, the punter approached the priest. 'Father,' he said, 'how is it the first two horses won but not the third?'

The priest looked sternly at him: 'That's the trouble with you Protestants,' he said, 'you can never tell the difference between a Blessing and the Last Rites.'

* * * * *

H.G. Wells once said of Catholics:

Confession on Saturday,
Absolution on Sunday,
At it again on Monday!

* * * * *

A chemist's shop was broken into and everything was stolen except the haircream and the contraceptives. The police are looking for a bald Catholic.

There is an old riddle which runs: 'What is it that God never sees, Kings and Queens see seldom and we see every day?'

A schoolboy, after thinking hard, replied: 'A joke.'

Two Evidence Guild speakers were discussing this and one said, 'The boy was right. A joke implies an incongruity and with God nothing is incongruous, therefore God cannot see a joke.'

'But,' replied the other, 'a sense of humour is perfection in man. Christ was a perfect man and therefore he must have been able to see a joke. But he was also God. Ergo – God can see a joke.'

'I see,' replied the first. 'Then every time a joke is told, the Second Person of the Blessed Trinity has to explain it to the other two.'

* * * * *

A boy at school stubbornly maintained that there were only six sacraments instead of seven, and explained that his father had taught him that Matrimony and Penance were one and the same thing.

* * * * *

A man fell in love with and married a practising Catholic girl. Although he was himself an agnostic, he had no objection at all to her continuing her devotions and bringing the children up in her faith. The only thing which did annoy him was the way she would pester him to come to Church. Having resisted her persuasions for some twenty years, he gave in one Sunday, although weakly protesting that he would not know what to do. She dismissed this objection by telling him that she would give instructions to him throughout. During the first half-hour she was persistently whispering 'stand-up' . . . 'kneel' . . .

'cross yourself' … 'sit down' … and so on, until he adopted that half-crouch position popular with reluctant churchgoers. On observing him in this position, she turned to him and asked: 'What's the matter, are your flies undone?'

Looking with great embarrassment the poor fellow replied: 'No, they're not. Should they be?'

*   *   *   *   *

In the fictitious school of Dunmere in his novel *George Brown's Schooldays*, Bruce Marshall shows that a certain amount of confusion in its religious teaching existed in the teaching staff:

'The teaching of the Church on the matter is quite final,' said Mr Saracen to his confirmation class. 'Hell really exists but not the traditional hell of fire and brimstone imagined by the Fathers of the Church who were ignorant men misled by the primitive chronology of their day … Hell is a state, not a place, and its pains are spiritual rather than physical.'

'Whatever so-called modern thought may say to the contrary, hell is a definite place in space, the pains of hell are physical and the agent by which they are inflicted is fire,' said Mr Martin to his confirmation class on the floor above. 'In hell men burn for ever and the flames which torture them never go out. The most appalling pains endured in torture chambers are nothing compared to the agonies suffered by the damned in hell. Hell, then, is a place.'

In his study, the Headmaster was instructing his confirmation class. 'Hell, either as a place or a state, exists only in the minds of retrograde theologians. In other words, hell does not exist at all.'

'But sir,' said Winkman, 'last year you told us that it was

quite possible that hell was a place but that nobody knew exactly where it was.'

'Then I must have told you wrongly,' said the Headmaster who sometimes changed his mind on these matters.

*   *   *   *   *

The bishop often wished that he found it a little easier to love his clergy, but supposed that he saw too much of them for that: St James seemed to have got things wrong when he said that a man who didn't love his brother whom he had seen couldn't possibly love God whom he hadn't seen: surely it was precisely because man had seen his brother that he found him so difficult to love.

*   *   *   *   *

Methodist minister: You Catholics don't really believe in Purgatory, do you?
Catholic priest: Well, you might go further and fare worse.

*   *   *   *   *

Martin Luther became increasingly irritated by the cool, calm virtue and restraint shown by his friend and follower Phillip Melancthon, the author of the Augsberg Confession. One day he lost patience. 'For heaven's sake,' he roared, 'why the devil don't you go out and sin a little? If you are to be forgiven by God you must have sinned first.'

*   *   *   *   *

'Sir, the pretending to extraordinary revelations and gifts of the Holy Ghost is a horrid thing, a very horrid thing.'

–Anon.

'I've been sixty years in this world,' said a man to Father Healey, 'and I have never been able to tell the difference between a good Protestant and a good Catholic.'

'You won't be sixty seconds in the next world,' was the reply, 'before you'll know the difference.'

*   *   *   *   *

'Why did Our Lord, after his Resurrection, first appear to the Holy Women?' asked a scholar who had a low opinion of the fair sex.

The apologist, after scratching his head, replied, 'Our Lord acted wisely in the circumstances because he knew that that was the fastest way to spread the news.'

*   *   *   *   *

A devoted missionary priest on a cannibal island had retired. Just before he died, he paid a return visit to see his flock and found that they had reverted to cannibalism and had only the day before enjoyed a long cannibal feast. Dreadfully saddened, he sought out the young man who had been an altar boy and one of his best converts. 'You didn't take part in this cannibal feast, did you?' he asked.

'No, of course not, Father, how could I? It was Friday.'

*   *   *   *   *

'Heaven is the place where the donkey at last catches up with the carrot.'

–Anon.

The Protestant Heresies

'It is not easy for a Protestant and a Catholic to lie in the same bed unless both are asleep.'

*   *   *   *   *

A young Catholic girl became engaged to a Protestant boy and asked all her relatives to pray for his conversion. Within a month her prayers were answered when the boy announced his intention of getting instruction and becoming a Catholic. Things went happily for some months, the boy continued his instruction, was received and all hoped that he would become and stay a good convert. One day, the girl rushed to her family in great distress. 'Stop praying,' she said, 'the prayers are working too well. Now he wants to become a priest.'

*   *   *   *   *

During unfortunate Irish riots, a Catholic was found dead in the street with forty-five bullet rounds in his body. The coroner, who was a Protestant, said at the inquest that it was the worst case of suicide he'd ever come across.

*   *   *   *   *

The Catholic priest of a small parish village was amazed to hear that Paddy, the most devout of all his flock, had on his death-bed been converted to Protestantism. He hurried to the house to confirm the news. 'Why the change?' he asked the dying man.

Paddy answered: 'Sure now, Father, as me time is up, I

thought it better that one of them should go rather than one of us.'

*   *   *   *   *

What is the Catholic definition of a contraceptive?

Something which a Protestant uses on every conceivable occasion.

*   *   *   *   *

A Catholic priest and a local vicar were having tea together in the priest's house. 'We may have the better halves,' said the vicar looking round appreciatively, 'but you have the better quarters.'

*   *   *   *   *

'You Catholics,' said the Protestant disgustedly, 'you go round burning heretics.'

'Nonsense,' said the Catholic, 'we just warm them up a little.'

*   *   *   *   *

Two Protestant Belfast dockworkers, Sam and Dave, were having their tea-break. Sam unfolded the morning paper. 'See here, Dave,' he said, 'they just elected a new Pope.'

Dave nodded his head gloomily. 'Aye,' he said, 'and I bet you a hundred pounds to a penny it was a bloody Catholic got the job.'

*   *   *   *   *

A Belfast Protestant, seeing a Catholic shop full of sacred hearts, crucifixes, saintly images and missals, picked up a stone and hurled it through the window, saying: 'Jesus Christ, I can't stand all this bloody intolerance.'

* * * * *

A Catholic woman looked disgusted as a High Anglican Protestant clergyman passed her in the streets: 'Calls himself a Father, and him with a wife and six kids.'

* * * * *

A former Archbishop of Dublin once decreed that it would be a mortal sin for any Catholic to enter the Protestant Trinity College, Dublin, without his express approval. A certain Catholic committed this sin. When he died, he presented himself to St Peter who sternly refused him admission, explaining to God that he had gone to Trinity College without permission from the Archbishop. God gently waved Peter aside and led the poor man into Heaven, exclaiming, 'After all, I am a Trinity man myself.'

* * * * *

A little Catholic boy was great friends with a little Protestant girl. One hot day while walking by the sea they decided to undress and go swimming. The little boy kept looking at her with great puzzlement, and that evening he said to his mother when telling her about it: 'I didn't know there was such a difference between Catholics and Protestants.'

* * * * *

When James Joyce, a lapsed Catholic was asked if he intended to become a Protestant, he replied, 'I may have lost my faith, but I haven't lost my commonsense.'

The Irish priest was trying to stop a man jumping from the top of a tall office block to his death. 'For God's sake, don't do it,' he said.

'God can take care of himself,' said the man.

'For the sake of St Peter and all the Most Holy Saints, don't do it,' he said.

'They can take care of themselves,' replied the man.

'For the sake of the most Holy Virgin, don't do it.' Shouted the priest.

The man looked at him curiously. 'Holy Virgin, who's she?' he asked. The priest looked contemptuously at him.

'Jump, you dirty Protestant, jump.'

*   *   *   *   *

The Protestant and the Catholic padres were talking in the officers' mess over breakfast one day.

'I had the most amazingly vivid dream last night, Father,' said the Protestant padre, 'it was all about Heaven, and at the centre was God on a throne and grouped all around him were us, the members of the Church of England. Beyond us were all the Nonconformists, the Presbyterians, the Baptists, and the Methodists, and the others. Still further away were the lesser sects, Jehovah's witnesses, Christian Scientists, Seventh Day Adventists and the like. And far beyond them, so far away as to be practically invisible, were your lot, the Catholics. Funny wasn't it?'

'Not in the least,' said the Catholic priest. 'Mine are the only lot God can trust out of his sight.'

*   *   *   *   *

During the last war, Bootham, the Quaker School at York, was for a short time evacuated to Ampleforth, the Benedictine Catholic School, where it occupied what is now the Junior House building. On one occasion, the late

Father Paul Nevill, Ampleforth's famous headmaster, had to address the two schools assembled together, and wittily started his speech with the preamble: 'Friends, Romans and Countrymen . . .'

*   *   *   *   *

A Catholic soldier died in the absence of the Catholic padre, the Protestant padre buried him and read the Protestant burial service. The Catholic padre was furious when he returned and decided to put matters right. He strode to the cemetery, stood in the front of the grave, shouted 'As you were' and started to read the Requiem Mass.

*   *   *   *   *

A Catholic priest and a Protestant clergyman were having a heated argument over the merits of their respective faiths. Neither would agree nor yield a point to the other. Finally the Catholic gave it up, saying: 'Very well, we must agree to differ and go our separate ways – you to worship God in your way and me to worship Him in His.'

*   *   *   *   *

Belfast Catholics are refusing to put R.I.P. on their tombstones any more. They say that it stands for 'The Reverend Ian Paisley'!

*   *   *   *   *

'I do hereby profess that Protestantism is the drearist of all religions; that the thought of the Anglican service makes me shiver and the thought of the 39 Articles makes me shudder.'

– Cardinal Newman (1801-1890)

23

A young Catholic farmer married a Protestant girl and after she presented him with a son, he converted her to the faith. He was middle-aged when she died, so he married another Protestant girl who, after presenting him with another son, was converted to the faith and died. By this time the farmer was getting on in years and again he married a Protestant girl but after a year she was not only not pregnant but not Catholic either. So the priest went down to see him and said: 'Now, Patrick, I have put up with your marrying all these Protestant girls because you convert them fairly fast, but it doesn't seem to be working out with the latest one. What's the trouble?'

'Well, Father,' he replied with a sheepish smile, 'I'm getting old, and the old converter isn't what it used to be.'

*   *   *   *   *

A priest is driving his car in Ireland and he sees a couple of Orangemen from over the border walking down the road wearing their orange sashes. The priest is so angry at this sight that he drives into them: one goes through the windscreen and the other is sent flying into a ditch. A local guard rushes up.

'Are ye all right, Father?' he asks.

'Sure I'm all right, but what about these fellers?'

The guard looks pityingly at them and shakes his head. 'Don't ye be worryin' about them, Father,' he says. 'That feller through the windscreen we'll have for breakin' and enterin', and as for the feller in the ditch, we'll get him for leavin' the scene of the accident.'

*   *   *   *   *

A Protestant woman rang a priest in the middle of the night and demanded to be received into the Catholic faith immediately.

'What's the hurry?' he asked.

'I've had a terrible row at home,' she told him, 'and I'm determined to disgrace the family.'

*   *   *   *   *

During the Eucharistic Congress in Chicago in the 1920s, Cardinal Spellman – America's most famous Cardinal – was driving his car at full speed. Not recognising him, an Irish policeman stepped out into the road, furious, and stopped the car. He was about to complain angrily about the bad driving when he realised who was sitting in the car. He saluted. 'Begging your pardon, Your Eminence, I just wanted to tell you that there is a Protestant policeman at the next corner.'

*   *   *   *   *

In Londonderry, a guard was controlling the traffic at a cross-roads and with the aid of his baton was calling to the people to cross in safety. 'Pedestrians, pedestrians,' he called, but a little old lady remained firmly at the kerb. Irritated, the guard went over to speak to her. *'I said pedestrians.'*

'Glory be to God, I heard you,' she replied. 'Perhaps you'll tell me when the Catholics can get across.'

*   *   *   *   *

Did you hear of the Catholic farmer who said he would die rather than be buried in a Protestant cemetery?

*   *   *   *   *

'I've got a wonderful job,' said Paddy to his mates. 'I'm knocking down a Protestant Church – and they're actually paying me to do it.'

Soon after the outbreak of the war, Paddy came from Ireland and obtained a job as a stoker in a munitions factory. So well did he do the job that he was given promotion: stoker at a newly opened crematorium at a far higher wage. Returning to his village he regaled his friends with stories of what he was doing in England. Talking of the crematorium job, he said: 'The joke of it all is that I'd do the job for nothing.'

'Why would you do it for nothing, Paddy?'

'Of course I would – burning Protestants.'

*   *   *   *   *

A classic Irish joke concerns two farmers who were waiting for the local Protestant landlord to pass by so that they could ventilate his hide with buckshot. It took him a long time to arrive. A terrible thought occurred to Mick.

'Paddy,' he said, 'say a prayer that nothing's happened to the poor man.'

*   *   *   *   *

The Wicked Protestant landlord robbed the poor farmer's daughter of her virtue and got her pregnant, but he wanted to be just. He sent for the girl's mother.

'Mrs Sullivan, you must know I can't marry your daughter but I wish to compensate her. I'll settle £5,000 on the child and give a further £2,000 to your daughter. For yourself, I have £500.'

She started to leave, a bit out of breath.

'The blessing of the revolving Indian saint of Inishbofin be on you, the blessing of the Holy Hermits of Clonmacnoise fall on you and all who belong to you . . .'

She paused. An awful thought struck her.

'Oh, heavens, milord . . . if she has a miscarriage will you give her another chance?'

A rich American attending a dinner party in England was making polite conversation with a titled Catholic lady next to him.

Lady: And what Church do you belong to?

Gentleman: Madam, I am a South Carolina Baptist.

Lady: Er, er . . . that's Low Church, isn't it?

Gentleman (cheerfully): Madam, you have no idea how low.

*   *   *   *   *

The Roman Catholic Archbishop of Leeds had been operated on by the late Lord Moynihan, who had given him a blood transfusion. The end was near and Lord Moynihan paid a visit to his patient to say goodbye.

Archbishop: Well, Moynihan, I know that I am dying. I have lived what I believe to have been a useful and active life and I am leaving this world with only one regret.

Moynihan: And what might that be?

Archbishop: I am very sorry that I have not been able to convert you to Roman Catholicism.

Moynihan: Well, my dear fellow, if you have not succeeded in converting me to your Catholic heresies, at least I have sent you to meet your Maker with some good Protestant blood in your veins.

*   *   *   *   *

Wee Jamie in Glasgow takes a box full of kittens to the Presbyterian minister.

Jamie: Would yer like tae buy m' ki'ens, mister? They're oful nice, an' genuine Pro'estan' ki'ens, genuine Rangers suppor'ers.

Minister: Och away wi'yer, Jamie. Yer cannae have Pro'estant ki'ens, an' wayll yooo know'!

A week later, Jamie takes the same kittens to his own priest.

Jamie: Would yer like t'buy me ki'ens, Father? They're oful nice, an' genuine Catholic ki'ens, real Celtic suppor'ers.

Priest: Now then, Jamie. I've been told that las' wik y'were tryin' tae sell them t'Mr MacCulloch as Pro'estan' ki'ens.

Jamie: Och aye, Father, tha' was las' week. Since then their eyes have opened.

*   *   *   *   *

Two old ladies were sitting in a park in Dublin, when in the distance they saw a black figure feeding the birds.

'Look at that,' said one. 'Isn't it lovely to see the Cardinal feeding the little birds, God's little creatures?'

'That's not the Archbishop,' replied the other, 'it's the Protestant man.'

'Oh,' retorted the first, 'all them t'housands o' people starvin' in the world, an' he's chockin' down bread in the streets!'

*   *   *   *   *

Two old ladies were sitting in a park in Dublin, when in the distance they saw a black figure walking with a poodle on a lead.

'Look at that, Monica,' said one, 'there's His Eminence taking the little dog for a walk. Isn't that lovely?'

'Yer want t'put yer glasses on, Mary,' replied the other. 'That's not the Cardinal ... it's the Protestant Archbishop.'

'Oh,' retorted the first old lady, 'the lazy divil! Why doesn't he get on with some work!'

*   *   *   *   *

Some years ago an elderly Catholic lady from Dublin visiting London for the first time, wandered by mistake into Westminster Abbey instead of the Cathedral. Describing the experience to her family on her return, she said, 'I knew I'd come to the wrong place because I understood every word the priest was saying.'

The Papacy

The late Pope John XXIII was due to receive Mrs Jacqueline Kennedy in private audience. Normally, he didn't bother with protocol, but on this occasion he showed signs of anxiety. 'How does a Pope address the wife of the President of the United States?' he asked his Master of Protocol, who replied: 'Your Holiness, either Madame la President or Madam; but if Your Holiness wishes to be particularly informal, you can call her Mrs Kennedy.'

The Pope was heard to mutter these over to himself rather nervously. When she arrived, he rushed towards her, impulsively kissed her on both cheeks and said, '*Aahhh, my darling Jackie!*'

*   *   *   *   *

'How many people work here in the Vatican?' asked a visitor. Pope John XXIII shrugged his shoulders and smiled:

'About half of them.'

*   *   *   *   *

One evening Pope John XXIII was dining at a foreign embassy in Rome. Included among the guests was a large, handsome woman who was wearing a dress which could only be described as scandalously low-cut. Everybody wondered what the Pope would say, but he made no comment and spoke to the woman with his usual charming friendliness.

At the end of the meal he took an apple and handed it to her. She was a little surprised by this unexpected gesture and asked him the reason for it. 'Madam,' he said with a gentle smile, 'it was only after Eve had taken the apple that she realised how little she was wearing.'

*   *   *   *   *

The Pope had just been elected and the head of the Papal staff, a very old Monsignor, took him on a tour of the Vatican Palace. A locked iron door led to a steep staircase which eventually led into a gloomy cellar in the middle of which stood a huge iron chest of unimaginable antiquity covered with rust and cobwebs. 'It's been there for two thousand years, ever since St Peter,' whispered the Monsignor. 'St Peter evidently left behind strict instructions that on no account was it to be opened. I don't know what's inside, nobody does.'

The Pope ordered it to be opened. 'No please, Your Holiness,' said the Monsignor anxiously, 'please don't. I have a feeling that it would be disastrous if you opened it.' The Pope was adamant, a locksmith was sent for. After a lot of trouble, and with much sighing of rusty hinges, the chest was opened. It was empty except for a small piece of paper folded in two and lying on a rusty metal plate. The Pope took the paper and looked at it.

It was the bill for the Last Supper.

*   *   *   *   *

VAT 69. The Pope's telephone number?

*   *   *   *   *

The Archbishop of Canterbury had an audience with the Pope:
Archbishop: Hi, Pope.
Pope: . . .'lo, church!

31

A news-reader in the Vatican Radio Service broadcasting to the French colonies meant to say 'la population immense du Cape', but instead committed the greatest Spoonerism in broadcasting (not to say Papal) history when he said *'la copulation immense du Pape'*.

*　　*　　*　　*　　*

'Short of showing Shakespeare round Stratford on Avon, I would dearly love to show Jesus Christ round the Vatican.'
– Malcolm Muggeridge

*　　*　　*　　*　　*

In a rather thoughtless moment the Vatican announced that there were, in fact, 143 officially recognised sins. The news spread like wildfire round the world, and the Press Officer was swamped with thousands of letters eagerly asking for a copy of the complete list.

*　　*　　*　　*　　*

Irish pilgrimage leader to Pius XII: Holy Father, there's not a man here who wouldn't be willing to go through hell-fire for you.

*　　*　　*　　*　　*

When Britain's John Freeman conducted his famous series of television interviews, 'Face to Face', and finally succeeded in arranging one with Pope John XXIII, it was perhaps inevitable that this should be known as 'Faith to Faith'.

*　　*　　*　　*　　*

Many years ago the Anglican Bishop of Gibraltar, whose parish embraced most of the Mediterranean, had an audience with the Pope who greeted him with: 'I believe I am in your Lordship's diocese?'

*　　*　　*　　*　　*

The Archbishop of Canterbury meeting the Pope in 1960 – the first time in four hundred years – shortly after the *Lady Chatterley's Lover* trial at the Old Bailey: 'Banned any good books lately?'

*　　*　　*　　*　　*

'I must believe in the Apostolic Succession: there is no other way of explaining the descent of the Bishop of Exeter from Judas Iscariot.'
　　　　　　　　　　　– Sydney Smith (1771-1845)

*　　*　　*　　*　　*

Pope John, when still a nuncio in Paris, once visited a convent in Belgium. A very tall sister was presented to him.
　'Please pray for me,' she asked.
　'You are so much nearer to heaven than I,' replied the Pope, '*you* must please pray for me.'

*　　*　　*　　*　　*

Pope Alexander VI, one of the Borgias, was asked on his death-bed (1503) whether he had forgiven all his enemies.
　'I have no enemies,' he said calmly. 'I have killed them all.'

*　　*　　*　　*　　*

In 1857, the Reverend David Hargreaves, an Anglican Minister, made a journey to the Vatican and succeeded in obtaining an audience with the Pope in order to discuss the subject of ecumenism which, in the middle of the nineteenth century, did not enjoy the same popularity it does now. It was with reluctance that the Pope consented to receive an Anglican clergyman, whom he naturally regarded as a complete heretic, and it was with some anger that he heard Hargreaves's request at the end of the audience for a blessing. The Pope gave him the blessing but it was in the form used when blessing incense at High Mass: *I belo benedicaris in cujus honore cremevellis* (May he bless you in whose honour you will burn).

* * * * *

When abstinence on Fridays was still a Law of the Church, the wartime Pope, Pius XII, ruled that whalemeat could be regarded as fish.

Punch's comment was: 'Ah well, one man's meat is another man's poisson.'

* * * * *

'The Pope is barely Catholic enough for some converts.'
– John Aycough (1858-1928)

* * * * *

The Pope's greeting to the Archbishop of Canterbury: 'Aahhh, my Lord Archbishop, long time no Holy See . . .'

* * * * *

A famous *grande-dame* was converted to Rome while at St Peter's and thereafter became an ardent and proselytising Catholic, gathering in prospective converts from field and

34

hedgerow. At one point she decided to seek an audience with His Holiness Pope Pius XII. Not having made a previous appointment, the Papal Chamberlain was most reluctant to make the necessary arrangements, but the forceful lady was insistent and eventually had her own way. At the door to the Papal apartment, the Chamberlain gave her some friendly words of advice: 'You must remember that His Holiness is very tired and I can only allow you twenty minutes.'

The audience duly commenced, the Chamberlain waiting outside the door. Twenty minutes passed, then forty, without any sign of the visitor taking her leave. After fifty minutes the Chamberlain began to get most anxious, and, after furtively looking around to ensure that no one was watching, he applied his eye to the keyhole. The lady was seated on a low stool before the Papal throne animatedly talking to His Holiness and gesticulating for emphasis, whilst Pius could be seen slumped in the great chair, his head in his hands. At last the tired, elegant, patrician voice floated through to the eavesdropping Chamberlain: 'But madam – I must tell you that I already *am* a Catholic! . . .'

*   *   *   *   *

Pope John XXIII said to *The Times*: 'Often, when I am near sleep and there is something worrying me, I find myself saying that I must talk to the Pope about it. And then I realise that I am the Pope. And this wakes me up.'

*   *   *   *   *

Winston Churchill said of Pope Pius XII, 'He could see a joke only by appointment.'

*   *   *   *   *

In Darkest Africa it was once customary for travellers to carry a medical card which said, 'I am a very important Catholic. In case of serious illness or accident, please inform the Pope.'

*　　*　　*　　*　　*

'The first ten commandments are the hardest' was Pope John XXIII's advice to converts.

*　　*　　*　　*　　*

Best Salesman of the Year? The man who sold a double-bed to the Pope!

*　　*　　*　　*　　*

Howard Dietz, the American lyric writer, while still at college, was asked with the other students to produce the shortest headline which would have the greatest shock appeal. He won the prize with 'Pope elopes.'

*　　*　　*　　*　　*

Rhythm method? Another name for Vatican Roulette.

*　　*　　*　　*　　*

The Chief Rabbi was talking to the Pope.
　'Why don't you let your flock take the birth control pill?'
　'That's simple,' replied the Pope. 'We don't want to let you catch us up.'

*　　*　　*　　*　　*

Pope John XXIII received a crate of bottles of cherry brandy, for which he was known to have a weakness. 'I like

your gift of fruit to me,' he said, 'but more than anything
else I appreciate the spirit in which it has been offered.'

*   *   *   *   *

Napoleon imprisoned Pius VII and Cardinal Consalvi, his
Secretary of State, in an attempt to push them into giving
him a divorce from Josephine. Both prelates proved to be
extremely stubborn: one day the exasperated Emperor
banged his fist on the table and roared at the Pope,
'Eminence, Holy Father, don't you realise I can destroy
this Church of yours?'

'On the contrary, Your Highness,' replied the Pope, 'you
cannot. We priests have been trying to do just that for 1800
years and so far we haven't succeeded.'

*   *   *   *   *

The Vatican has hired a trendy new designer to bring the
domestic arrangements up to date. The handbasins in the
lavatories now have three taps, Hot, Cold and Holy.

*   *   *   *   *

An American big-business President was granted an
audience with the Pope. It dragged on for hours. Outside
the door, a group of worried Cardinals were listening
through the keyhole wondering what was taking place.

'I'm sorry, Mr Hackenschmidt, but it's quite impossi-
ble,' they heard the Pope say.

'Ten million dollars and that's my final offer. Ten million
dollars *a year*,' said the American.

'No, it's out of the question.'

The door opened and the American walked out seething
with anger and frustration. After a pause, the Cardinals
entered and asked the Pope how he could refuse ten million

dollars a year in view of the terrible poverty in Italy. 'What did the American want?' they asked.

'Something I could not give him,' said the Pope firmly. 'He wanted me to rewrite the Lord's Prayer to include the words, "Give us this day our daily Crispy Crunchy Doughnuts."'

*   *   *   *   *

Flying back to Paris after the Papal Election, the French Cardinal was in a bad temper. Firstly, the coffee was cold. Secondly, he was still a Cardinal.

– *Every Man a Penny*, Bruce Marshall

*   *   *   *   *

A very talkative and boring barber asked a customer whether he had taken his holidays yet.

'I leave in a fortnight.'

'Where are you going?'

'Italy.'

'You'll visit Rome, I suppose.'

'Yes.'

'And see the Pope?'

'If an opportunity presents itself.'

A month later the same customer returned for his usual haircut.

'Have a good holiday?'

'Very good.'

'Weather all right?'

'Quite sunny.'

'Did you go to Rome?'

'Yes.'

'See the Pope?'

'Yes. And he spoke to me.'
'*Really?* What did he say?'
'The Pope said, "Where on earth did you get such a terrible haircut?" '

The Arts

While I was on the Queen Mary I had an invitation to have a drink with Graham Greene in the second-class bar. Second-class! He was a very wealthy man and could well have afforded first class, so why second? He was a good Catholic boy, so what mortal sin could he possibly have committed for which the only possible expiation was to travel second-class on the Queen Mary? When I got there I found him in a rather depressed mood: his latest novel had not sold well, the bottom had clearly fallen out of the market, he would write no more religious novels.

'Oh, I shouldn't give up writing about God if I were you,' I said. 'It's rather like Plum Wodehouse dropping Bertie Wooster half way through the Jeeves series.'

To console him I suggested that we write a Catholic novel in collaboration and after a couple of bottles of Moet & Chandon we concocted a plot which dealt with a music-loving, sports-loving young blonde priest who goes to Ampleforth as games-master, and organist. He falls passionately in love with the Head Boy, a hairy-chested muscular young brute, who happens also to be Captain of Boxing and Captain of Rugger. They commit the sin of sodomy in the priest's bedroom and are so tormented by feelings of guilt, an awareness of mortal sin and a dread of eternal hellfire that they commit double suicide . . . in front of the altar . . . on Good Friday . . . during High Mass . . . in the presence of the Cardinal of Westminster, the Archbishop of Canterbury and the Chief Rabbi.

'You write it, Graham old boy,' I said, 'it's very much your style.'

'Oh no, I couldn't possibly,' he said giggling with nervous embarrassment, 'you write it, Evelyn.'

So we tossed for it and he won. I never discovered if he ever did write it or not. I hope he did.

> – *A Talent to Abuse* (play), Richard Huggett

*　　*　　*　　*　　*

The success of *St Joan* was immediate and lasting on its first production in 1923. So deep was Shaw's understanding of Catholic dogma and the Church's views on heresy that many people thought this indicated a change of heart in his well-known atheistic views. An old lady came to him shortly after the premiere and said: 'I hope this means, Mr Shaw, that you are now going to become a Catholic?'

Shaw's reply was swift: 'Certainly not, madam, there's not enough room in the world for two popes.'

*　　*　　*　　*　　*

The last of the great religious blockbusters was an epic film called *King of Kings,* a biography of Jesus Christ, with Jeffrey Hunter starring as Christ and Siobhan McKenna playing Mary, his mother. A number of alternative titles were bandied round Catholic circles:

Carry On, Jesus . . . Rock Around The Cross . . . Jesus, was your mother born in Ireland? . . . Breakfast at Epiphany . . . and *Suddenly, Last Supper.*

*　　*　　*　　*　　*

Amanda: Do you realise we're living in sin?

Elyot: Not according to the Catholics. They don't recognise divorce. According to them we're still legally married.

Amanda: But we're not Catholics.

Elyot: No, but it's nice to feel that they might back us up.

Amanda: Well, we may be all right in the sight of heaven, but socially we're still in a hell of a mess.

> – *Private Lives*, Noël Coward

'The Creator made Italy from designs by Michaelangelo.'

'In every fat priest there is always a bony martyr crying out for beatitude.'

'There is no stink in the world that can compare with the odour of sanctity.'

'The vestigial nipples of man are about as useful as the papal pudenda.'

— *Hadrian the Seventh*, Peter Luke

*   *   *   *   *

'Be it never so lustful, there's no place like Rome.'
— Kenneth Tynan's review of *The Living Room*, Grahame Greene

*   *   *   *   *

'...I was riveted by the spectacle of these two expert performers, Sir Donald Wolfit and Mr Ernest Milton, stealthily upstaging each other for the greater glory of God.'

Review of *The Strong Are Lonely*

*   *   *   *   *

The present Pope, John Paul II, was an actor before he became a priest. He also wrote a play, *The Jeweller's Shop*. As an amazing act of piety and courtesy it was presented in London at the Westminster Theatre to coincide with his official papal visit to London in the Summer of 1982.

The notices were astonishingly kind and it had a respectable run of nearly five months, being attended largely by the Catholic clergy and large parties of schoolchildren from Catholic schools, but all the respect and goodwill couldn't disguise the fact that it was a terrible bore. Satirical comment abounded in the London press, of which this piece by Miles Kington is a good example.

THE TALKING SHOP
A new papal play

Scene: An exit from a theatre. Two critics exit from the theatre.

1st Critic: What is your serious opinion of the very serious drama we have just seen?

2nd Critic: It is a play written by a man whom I would consider to be a very great man indeed, and a very holy man, for an evening in the theatre lasts only two hours but holiness lasts for ever.

1st Critic: This, though an answer to a question, is not the answer to the question I have just uttered. You are a man who loves the theatre. Do you love this play?

2nd Critic: My love for the theatre encompasses all kinds of plays. When I was first called to the noble pursuit of drama criticism I did not expect that every play I would see would be a masterpiece, for a life composed entirely of masterpieces does not admit of the idea of imperfection. Should one not also see tedious plays? I think one should. Tediousness involves suffering, and suffering involves learning, and learning involves wisdom. . . (*he continues his monologue while the first critic starts his*).

1st Critic: This is very strange. When we entered the portals of this theatre my friend was not talking in this unaccustomed style, a veritable mixture of windy prose and old sermons. He was talking in a very different manner. 'Hi Jack,' he said. 'Time for a stiff one. We are going to need it. Tedium Laudamus, ha ha.' Those were his very words, for I have inscribed them in a little book I keep with me night and day, that I may study them in moments of reflection.

Yet here he is now sounding like an also-ran in the Nobel Translation Prize. And here I am addressing myself in much the same wise. I would that I might know what has happened to me.

2nd Critic: . . . and therefore love, and suffering, and going to the theatre, are one and the same thing. You were saying?

1st Critic: I was merely pondering on the fact that two hours in the theatre may also be seen as eternity.

2nd Critic: Eternity is not long enough for some thoughts.

1st Critic: There are many people who sleep through eternity and do not wake up to life.

2nd Critic: That is true. I myself dropped off for a while.

1st Critic: Ah, we seem to be getting back to normal.

2nd Critic: Though we have undoubtedly undergone a profound experience.

1st Critic: Or would have if we had been awake.

2nd Critic: True. But there now remains the great question that we must ask ourselves.

1st Critic: Namely, do we cast a damper on the papal visit by savaging his play as a piece of theatre?

2nd Critic: Or do we take the easy way out and say it is a good bit of Radio 3 by a very great man?

1st Critic: I think I shall mull this one over a quick drink.

2nd Critic: I wouldn't say no myself.

1st Critic: I wonder if Ronald Reagan has ever written a play?

2nd Critic: God be merciful. *They re-enter the theatre.*

*   *   *   *   *

The late Finlay Currie, the actor, once related that in the United States he met an American comedian who was planning a tour of the English music halls. When Finlay asked why Ireland was not included in his schedule, the comedian said that he thought the Irish audiences 'might

44

prove a little tricky.' Finlay strongly advised him to reconsider – which he did.

When they next met, the comedian was full of gratitude. 'You were quite right,' he said. 'The Irish audiences were absolutely marvellous, every one of them – Catholics and Christians alike.'

*   *   *   *   *

A priest in a small town had great difficulty in finding a boy to serve Mass until somebody suggested that he had a smart boy in the congregation who was also call boy at the local theatre. The boy was brought to him: he agreed to serve and was duly given instruction by the priest until the morning of his first Mass.

'Now go out to the altar, put on the lights, light the candles, take the wine and water and then tell me when everything is ready' said the priest.

The boy did all this and then returned to the door of the sacristy and, giving a loud knock, shouted, 'Overture and Beginners Please, Act One.'

*   *   *   *   *

A man travelling to Dublin from London on Aer Lingus starts a conversation with the man sitting next to him. 'Are you going for a holiday or for work?'

'I'm g-g-g-going for a job as an Announcer for Telefis Eireann,' was the reply. 'I have an aud-d-d-d-dition t-t-t-tomorrow m-m-m-morning.'
Two days later, by a curious coincidence, they met on the plane returning to London.

'Did you get the job?' asked the first man. 'No, I d-d-d-didn't,' was the sad reply. 'They said they n-n-n-n-needed a C-C-C-C-atholic.'

Sister Veronica of the Sacred Heart Convent, Wimbledon, wanted to get official guidance on a recently released film with a view to arranging a school party. 'Is that the Legion of Decency?' she asked when she finally got through.

'No, but you have the next best thing,' the voice answered, 'this is the Pure Oil Company.'

* * * * *

When I went to see the film *The Ten Commandments*, I noticed an eleventh:

THOU SHALT NOT SMOKE.

* * * * *

After the première of *Hadrian the Seventh*, Cardinal Heenan said to the Archbishop of Canterbury, 'Still want to join us?'

Catholics, Jews and Others

A priest and a rabbi met in a boxing stadium. The rabbi noticed that one of the boxers made the sign of the cross and said a little prayer just before the fight started. 'Father,' he said, 'will that help him?'

'Certainly it will,' said the priest, 'as long as he can fight.'

*   *   *   *   *

The rabbi, gazing across the road at the Roman Catholic church, shook his head in amazement at the large congregation, the priest's Rolls-Royce, and wondered how they managed it. He decided to send Heinz, one of his wardens, to spy on the service and find out the secret of the success of the Catholic Church. Heinz went to High Mass on the following Sunday and duly reported back to the rabbi. 'It's so simple,' he said. 'They start with a hymn and then the priest sings: "Who will play dominoes with me?" and the congregation all reply: "I will play dominoes with you," and then a couple of blokes go round with the silver plates collecting the side-bets!'

*   *   *   *   *

A Christian Scientist hailed a taxi in New York and asked the driver, a fervent Irish Catholic, to take him to the First Church of Christ. Instead, the driver took him to St Patrick's Catholic Cathedral.

'I said the First Church of Christ,' explained the Christian Scientist angrily.

'Say, Mac,' said the driver, 'if He's in town then He's right inside there.'

A priest was driving through a remote part of the country when suddenly his car broke down: he had no petrol so he was forced to walk to the nearest garage. The garage had no petrol can, and the only container available was an old chamber-pot. The priest was thus able to carry the petrol back to the car in the chamber-pot and to pour it into the tank.

A rabbi happened to be driving past and witnessed the scene. 'I always knew the Catholics had faith,' he said, 'but this is ridiculous.'

*　　*　　*　　*　　*

The Pope went to Israel and happened to be walking down the main street in a village where a Jewish shoe-shop and a Catholic shoe-shop faced each other in permanent rivalry. Suddenly, the strap on his sandal broke and he went into the Jewish shoe-shop to have it mended. The owner, deciding to get as much publicity as he could out of the visit, decided, the next day, to put a notice in the window: COBBLERS TO THE POPE. The following day the Catholic shop had a notice in its window: BALLS TO THE CHIEF RABBI.

*　　*　　*　　*　　*

The following line was written over a tunnel outside Cork:
Jew and Gentile may enter here but not a Papist.

Underneath somebody had written:
The man who wrote this wrote it well
For the same is written o'er the gate of Hell.

*　　*　　*　　*　　*

Cardinal Vaughan once sat next to the Chief Rabbi at a public dinner. In a jocular mood, the Cardinal said to the Chief Rabbi: 'When may I offer you a slice of this most excellent ham?'

The Rabbi replied: 'At Your Eminence's wedding.'

* * * * *

It was the wettest night of the year when Paddy collapsed in the streets of Dublin. 'Fetch the rabbi quickly,' he said to his friend, 'I'm dying.'

The friend said: 'And what would a good Catholic like you be wanting with a rabbi?'

Paddy said, 'Well, you wouldn't expect poor Father Murphy to come out on a night like this, would you?'

* * * * *

A Catholic bookmaker died and was given a big funeral. His wife attended with her husband's partner, who was Jewish. 'What do you think are the chances of Jack getting into heaven?' she asked.

'I don't know, he was a pretty tough fellow, but he gave quite a bit to charity; let's say fifty-fifty.'

'Only fifty-fifty?' said the wife in surprise. 'You know, Manny, he was very good to me and the kids.'

'Well,' Manny said, 'perhaps a little better than evens.'

When they reached the cemetery, the coffin was brought out and the party assembled beside the grave. The priest raised his hands to intone the blessing, and Manny, recognising the gesture, turned to the wife. 'Did you see those odds?' he whispered. 'He's slipped into the lead, it's odds on the favourite.'

* * * * *

A Jewish boy of ten was the despair of his parents. He was rude and surly; he was untidy in the home and always late for meals; he never washed and his school work was terrible. In despair his parents sent him to the local Catholic school to see if that would do anything for him. The effect was startling and miraculous. Overnight, everything changed. He washed, was punctual for meals, insisted on helping his mother with the housework, was well-mannered and good-humoured with everybody, and his work at school showed a dramatic improvement. His parents couldn't understand it, so one day they asked him why he had changed.

'Well, it's easy to explain. I went to this school and the woman in the black and white uniform took me inside this huge hall with rows of benches and statues and an organ. And at the far end, high up on the wall, there was this statue of the Jewish boy nailed by the hands and feet to a big wooden cross. They don't mess about in the Catholic schools.'

*　　　*　　　*　　　*　　　*

'My parish priest is much wiser than your rabbi,' said the little Catholic boy to the little Jewish boy. 'Of course he is,' was the reply, 'you tell him everything in that confessional.'

*　　　*　　　*　　　*　　　*

A Catholic and a Jew were standing next to each other in a Catholic church. As the collection plate was coming round, the Catholic said to the Jew, 'When it gets near us, you faint and I'll carry you out.'

*　　　*　　　*　　　*　　　*

The oldest lad of a Jewish family was almost eighteen and his parents were anxious to know what sort of a man he would become and so they set him a little test. On his birthday they took a Bible, a £5 note and a bottle of whisky and placed them in his room. If he read the Bible then he would become a rabbi, if he chose the money, a financier, but if he drank the whisky he was destined to become a waster all his life. When he went to his room his parents watched him through the keyhole. First of all he picked up the Bible and read a few passages, next he pocketed the £5 note, and finally he swigged the whisky. His father wrung his hands in despair and turned to his wife. 'Heaven help us, he is going to become a Roman Catholic priest!'

*   *   *   *   *

A Jewish gentleman was so enchanted by the spectacle of the local parish priest saying Mass and preaching his Easter sermon, that he asked to be received into the Catholic Church and to be baptised. This was done. On his return home he told his son that he was now a Catholic. 'Can you let me have £10 to take my girl to the pictures?'

The father obliged.

Next, his daughter entered the room, heard the good news and asked for £20 for a new dress.

Finally, his wife heard the news and asked for £100 for a new electric fire.

The father lost his temper and threw his wallet on to the floor.

'Not five minutes am I a Catholic,' he shouted, 'and already you dam' Jews are taking my money.'

*   *   *   *   *

In a small town there lived a successful Jewish business-man. Over the years he had developed a very warm friendship and close relationship with the local parish priest. One day they met in the street and Father Clancy said, 'Ben, I am glad to see you. You have been a steadfast friend over the years and whenever I needed a favour you have not hesitated. We are running short of funds for our school and we need £2,000 for new urinals.'

'Why not?' said Ben. 'I've had a good year and I'll take it off my income tax in any case.'

That night he was recounting the events of the day to his wife, and he happened to mention that he had given Father Clancy a cheque for some new urinals.

'What's that, urinals?' she asked.

'How should I know?' he answered. 'I'm not a Catholic.'

*   *   *   *   *

A Catholic priest and a rabbi were travelling alone in a train compartment, both very shy and desperately racking their brains for something to say. After many hours the priest said: 'Tell me, have you ever eaten pork?'

The rabbi looked alarmed, hung his head in shame and nodded. 'Yes,' he said.

Hours later he plucked up courage to speak to the priest. 'Tell me,' he said, 'have you ever committed adultery with a woman?'

The priest, even more alarmed, nodded and hung his head in shame.

Many hours passed in silence before the train arrived at its destination. The priest was the first to leave; as he descended to the platform, he turned and spoke rather gleefully to the rabbi.

'It's nicer than pork, isn't it?'

*   *   *   *   *

An English priest and a Jew were sharing a train compartment.

'You're a Catholic priest?' asked the Jew. 'What sort of prospects does that job hold?'

The priest answered: 'Eventually, if all goes well, I'll get a parish of my own.'

'What then?' asked the Jew.

'I might get made a canon.'

'Could you go further?'

'Yes, I suppose I could become a bishop.'

'And after that?'

'I might become an archbishop and after that I suppose I might even become a cardinal.'

'What next?'

'It's most unlikely, since there's only been one English Pope so far, but theoretically I could become Pope.'

The Jew considered this. 'Very good,' he said, 'and what then?'

The priest rather pityingly said: 'My dear fellow, really – what questions you ask. Beyond the Pope there is only God.'

'Well,' said the Jew rather smugly, 'one of our boys did it.'

The Pearly Gates

Two bishops died and went to Heaven. On their arrival at the Pearly Gates, St Peter bade them welcome. 'Gentlemen,' he said, 'Heaven is a big place so you will require transport. Here is a mini-car for your use during eternity.' As the bishops were about to get into the car, they noticed that a rabbi had arrived at the gates of Heaven and was given not another mini-car but a Rolls-Royce with a smartly-uniformed chauffeur. The rabbi drove off and the two bishops descended angrily on St Peter.

'We are the Princes of the One, True, Holy and Apostolic Church and he is only a rabbi. Why should he get a Rolls-Royce and not us?'

St Peter smiled. 'Well, your Eminences,' he said, 'it's the same up here as it is down on the Earth, you have to be nice to the boss's relatives!'

*   *   *   *   *

A priest went to visit an old man on his death-bed. In giving him the Last Sacraments, he asked him if he would renounce the Devil and all his Works. The old man looked worried. 'Wait a minute, Father,' he said, 'this isn't the time to be making enemies!'

*   *   *   *   *

A man arrived at the Pearly Gates and asked to be admitted. St Peter looked sternly at him and proceeded to question him about his earthly existence.

'Did you ever fornicate?'

'Certainly not!'

'Did you ever tell lies or cheat or steal?'
'No!'
'Did you ever smoke, drink or use bad language?'
'No, none of these things.'
'In that case,' said St Peter incredulously, 'if you've never done any of these things, tell me, what kept you so long?'

*　　　*　　　*　　　*　　　*

A man died and went to Heaven. When he arrived, St Peter met him and said he would show him around. They came to various groups sitting around Heaven. 'They're the Jews,' explained St Peter, 'those are the Protestants . . . those are the Muslims . . . over there are the Quakers. . . .'

Soon they came to a very large area surrounded by a high wall, from behind which they could hear the sounds of voices and laughter.

'Who are those people behind the wall?' asked the new arrival, curiously. 'Shussh,' replied St Peter, 'they are the Catholics, and they think they're the only ones here.'

*　　　*　　　*　　　*　　　*

Pet-lover to priest: Will we have our dogs in Heaven?
Priest: Certainly we will.
Pet-lover: But what about those who don't like animals?
Priest: That's all right; they won't be there.

*　　　*　　　*　　　*　　　*

A famous film producer went to Heaven and was asked by St Peter to make a film. 'You can have anybody you like,' said St Peter, 'all the famous stars, writers, directors, composers, artists, cameramen who are here, you can use them all.'

The producer was enraptured by the prospect. 'And the budget?' he enquired eagerly.

'The sky's the limit,' said St Peter.

'And there will be no censorship or front-office interference?' he asked.

St Peter shook his head. 'No, nobody will interfere, you can make any sort of film you like; all we ask is that it shall be good.'

The producer smiled happily. 'I'll get on to the casting department right away.'

St Peter took him gently aside. 'There is just one little thing I must tell you while you're on the subject of casting – there's a little angel that God's interested in. . . !'

*　　*　　*　　*　　*

This is a story about a little man, just an ordinary little man who went to heaven and found himself standing outside the Pearly Gates. Well, he looks up and finds St Peter standing next to him – anyway, he's on the welcoming committee. And St Peter says to him, 'Well,' he says, 'now you're in heaven and you have earned yourself eternal happiness.' 'Am I?' says the little man, 'have I really?' and St Peter says, 'you most certainly have, can't you hear the multitudes singing? Everybody is joyful. What do you say, my son?' So the little man takes a look round him at all the multitudes of the earth spread out against the universe and he says to St Peter, 'can I have a look, a proper look from where you're standing?' and St Peter says, 'of course you can, my son,' and the little man stands up where St Peter is and gazes at the Hosts of Heaven and all the rest of it.

'All the joy and wonder of eternity is around you,' says St Peter, 'what do you have to say?' and the little man looks round a bit more and says, 'all my life I've been wondering what I'd say if this ever happened to me, I couldn't think, somehow.' And St Peter smiles kindly and says: 'Well, my son, what do you say?' 'Only one thing,' says the little man – and he said it. Well, St Peter looks as if he'd been struck across the face by some great hand. The hosts stop singing, all the angels hide their faces in their wings and for a tiny splash in eternity there is no sound at all in Paradise. St Peter can't speak for a while and then he throws his arms round the little man and kisses him.

'I love you, my son,' he says, 'with all my heart I love you. Ever since I came here, I have been waiting to hear that word.'

– *The Entertainer,* John Osborne

*　　*　　*　　*　　*

Cardinal Spellman, America's most famous cardinal, died and went to Heaven. St Peter opened the pearly gates a chink and said: 'Yeeeeees, who are you?'

Spellman: Francis, Cardinal Spellman, Prince of the Church, although I like to think of myself as a simple parish priest with four million souls under my care.

St Peter: Oh? Just wait a moment. (*He returns after a lengthy period.*) I'm sorry, we don't seem to have you under prelates. Have you done anything else?

Spellman: Well, I have written one or two books of devotion and a novel which enjoyed a rather modest popular success.

St Peter: Oh? Do you mind waiting a bit? (*Again a lengthy pause. He returns.*) I'm so sorry, we don't seem to have your name listed under writers. Can you think of anything else?

Spellman: (*Now growing nervous.*) Well, I have built sixteen grammar schools, four high schools, one college, two orphanages, one home for the aged and a shelter for unmarried mothers.

St Peter: Oh, I see . . . terribly sorry to keep you waiting, but would you mind. . . (*Off he goes but this time returns almost immediately – all smiles!*) Come right in, Frankie, we had you listed under real estate agents!

*   *   *   *   *

When the Protestant clergy arrive in Heaven, the first thing that happens is Jesus Christ makes an introduction. 'I don't think you know my mother?'

*   *   *   *   *

Bill, George and John died and were halfway up the staircase to Heaven when they were stopped by St Peter.

St Peter: How many sins have you committed on Earth?

Bill: Not more than six. Or maybe seven. But no more.

St Peter: Very well, that's good. You can take the Cadillac and drive the rest of the way up to Heaven. How many sins did you commit, George?

George: About fifty. Not too bad for a lifetime, I fancy.

St Peter: I agree. You can take the Volkswagen. And what about you, John?

John: (ashamed) So many I've lost count. I'm sorry.

St Peter: Okay, since you're sorry, you can take the motorbike.

When they all arrived in Heaven, the boys laughed at John for being compelled to finish the journey by motorbike when the others had expensive cars.

'You think *that's* funny?' said John. 'I've just seen the Pope on a bicycle.'

*   *   *   *   *

A rabbi, a Methodist minister and a Catholic priest were standing at the Pearly Gates. Suddenly St Peter appears and says, 'As a reward for your good and virtuous behaviour on earth you are entitled to have one wish granted.'

Stepping forward, the rabbi says, 'I wish that there were no Protestants left on earth.' Next, the minister says, 'I wish there were no Jews left.'

After a pause, St Peter says, 'Well, Father, what do you wish?'

Without hesitation, the priest replies: 'I wish that you would grant them their wishes.'

*   *   *   *   *

One day Jesus woke up in Heaven and he felt tired, depressed, lethargic, and rather miserable. It was a typical Monday morning feeling, in fact. He wandered unhappily round Heaven looking for something or somebody to cheer him up and finally arrived at the Pearly Gates. He looked gloomily at the new arrivals. Suddenly, his attention was caught by an old man with a long beard whose face seemed familiar. He went up to him. 'Excuse me, but your face seems familiar. I'm sure we have met. What did you do down on earth?'

The old man smiled at him. 'As a matter of fact, I was a carpenter and lived a full and happy life until tragedy struck. My son left home and I never saw him again.'

Jesus looked at him with astonishment and delight. 'You were a carpenter and – let's get this right – your son left you and you never saw him again . . . Father, I am your son. Come and kiss me.'

The old man opened his eyes wide and rushed forward with his arms outstretched, crying '*Pinocchio!*'

*   *   *   *   *

One day Satan telephoned St Peter to say, 'I think there has been some mistake in your last consignment note, because we've just received a batch of ladies from the Catholic Women's League.'

'I'll look into it as soon as I can,' replied St Peter, 'and I'll telephone you back as soon as I can.'

'Please, *please*, I beg of you, be quick about it. They've already raised enough money to have Hell air-conditioned!'

*   *   *   *   *

A Jesuit priest dies and goes to Heaven. As he passes through the Pearly Gates he is surprised, and highly flattered, to be received by millions of angels, all cheering, brass bands, flags, great excitement everywhere, and God the Father with his Son and his Mother advancing to meet him with big welcoming smiles.

'Well, I must confess that I didn't expect anything quite like this,' he said.

'There's a good reason, my son,' said God. 'Your order was founded four hundred years ago and so far you're the first Jesuit who's arrived here.'

Sins of the Flesh

The mediaeval church was obsessed with sex to a quite painful degree. Not only was the pleasure of the sexual act held to be sinful, but also the desire for a person of the opposite sex, even when unconsummated. In the eighth century, the Church began to develop the enormously strict system which ruled the Middle Ages. Not everybody realises how strict were the rules which controlled the sexual act even when performed with the marital relationship.

Thus, the sexual act must be performed in only one position and numerous penalties were prescribed for using variants, some calling for seven years of penance. Not content with this, the Church proceeded to cut down the number of days upon which even married couples might legitimately perform the sexual act. First, it was made illegal on Sundays, Wednesdays and Fridays, which effectively removed the equivalent of five months in the year. Then it was made illegal for forty days before Easter and forty days before Christmas, and for three days before attending communion. It was also forbidden from the time of conception to forty days after child-birth. It was, of course, forbidden during penance.

Marriage being, as can be seen, a contaminating influence, the Church refused to perform it at certain times of the year – Advent, part of Lent, the greater part of March, May and December. The Church also restricted the hours during which marriage could be celebrated. It first declared that marriage must take place in daylight and then later defined daylight as 8am till noon. Though the legal hours were extended in modern times, the penalty of any clergyman who commits the frightful crime of marrying a couple after the proper hour remains at fourteen years' penal servitude.

— *Sex in History,* Gordon Rattray Taylor (1954)

*　　　*　　　*　　　*　　　*

A young nun goes to Reverend Mother in the convent and announces with a touch of triumph that she is pregnant. Reverend Mother is horribly shocked. 'Who's done this terrible thing, child?' she asks.

The young nun smiles seraphically.

'Ah, tis all right Reverend Mother,' she replied. 'It was St Michael himself.'

'Nonsense, child. What makes you think it was him?'

The nun smiles in ecstasy. 'Ah, sure, didn't I see it in the back of his Y-fronts?'

*　　　*　　　*　　　*　　　*

Logarithm? A Catholic birth-control record.

*　　　*　　　*　　　*　　　*

You know what they call people who use the rhythm system of birth control? Parents.

*　　　*　　　*　　　*　　　*

Two public school boys who were always very sarcastic to each other grew up to become a tall thin admiral and a very fat bishop. One day, decades after they left school, they met at Plymouth Station. Even after thirty years they had no difficulty in recognising each other.

'Tell me, porter, where can I find the London train?' said the bishop.

'Platform three,' replied the admiral, 'but I'm very

surprised that a lady in your pregnant condition should be travelling alone to London.'

* * * * *

London society is full of people energetically pursuing a life of sin and bursting with frustration because there are only ten commandments to break.

* * * * *

The Catholic girl who married a Protestant boy got up at 6 a.m. on the first morning of the honeymoon to go to Mass. As a result of her husband's pleadings she got back into bed. Asked why she had changed her mind, she said, 'The Church of Rome will stand for ever, but I'm not so sure about some of the Protestant erections.'

* * * * *

Priest to Prostitute: I pray for you every night.
Prostitute to Priest: Well, there's really no need, Father, I'm on the telephone.

* * * * *

A Catholic took his sixteen children to the local cattle show to see the animals. He went up to a farmer and said, 'Excuse me, may I bring my kids to look at the prize bull?'

The farmer looked at him, and then at the sixteen children. 'Hang on,' he said. 'I'll bring the prize bull out to look at *you*.'

* * * * *

A priest new to his parish thought the best place to make friends would be in the local pub. He went along, bought a pint, but no one would speak to him. Eventually, after another drink, he needed the gents and was directed to it by the barman.

Inside the gents, to his astonishment, he found a large picture on the wall. Showing a naked women, it was entitled 'Eve', and there was a figleaf hanging on it. When he returned to the bar he was surprised that everyone turned round and started talking to him. So he asked why they had become friendly.

'Well,' the barman grinned, 'whenever anyone moves the figleaf a bell rings in the bar.'

*　　*　　*　　*　　*

'I want you to call out the banns for me and Maggie MacDonnell,' said Paddy to the priest.

'Aaaah, a grand wee girl,' says the priest.

'She'll make a grand wife, Father.'

'She surely will, what a figure.'

'She's a fine cook and a good churchgoer.'

'Yes, and so well made, what a figure.'

'But surely, Father, you're a celibate.'

'Of course I am, Paddy, but you can read the menu without having the lunch.'

*　　*　　*　　*　　*

The shrine of Sainte Anne de Beaupré in Quebec is known as the American Lourdes. There is a long and steep flight of stone steps to the church, and it is the punishing and painful penance of all pilgrims to climb this on their knees. A lady is doing this, but the heels of her shoes keep catching in her rather long skirt. She turns to the elderly gentleman following her. 'Would you be kind enough to lift up my dress a little?

64

The elderly gentleman replies: 'Madam, I will not. It is because I used to do just that that I am now making penance by doing this!'

*   *   *   *   *

A young priest, newly ordained, complained to the Father Superior of the order, an old man of ninety-five, that impure thoughts and sexual temptations came crowding into his mind at night, no matter how hard he tried to resist them. 'Father, how long does this go on? How old do you have to be before you are released from the lusts of the body?'

The aged priest gazed long and hard into the flickering fire and finally heaved a long sigh. 'I don't know,' he said.

*   *   *   *   *

Saint Augustine was one who found the lusts of the body particularly tormenting, as we learn from his Confessions. A famous version of his prayer, translated from the Latin, is as follows: 'Dear God, please make me virtuous and chaste – but not just yet.'

*   *   *   *   *

Paddy was a great drunkard, and so Father O'Flynn pays him a visit and advises him to mend his ways, give up drinking and pray to the Virgin Mary for help. That evening Paddy goes to church, falls to his knees and prays: 'Oh, Mary, Mother of God, if you give me a pound tonight I'll be a better man.'

Father O'Flynn slips a fifty-pence coin into his pocket, hoping this ploy would cure him.

'Where's my pound, Father?' asks Paddy, as he scrambles to his feet.

'Look in your pocket,ª my son,' says the priest.

Paddy does so and pulls out the fifty-pence coin. 'That's fine, Father, but it's a pound I'm wanting.'

'Never mind, Paddy, you come back tomorrow night, pray again and see what the Virgin Mary can do for you.'

Paddy goes to the village pub and gets rotten drunk on his fifty pence.

Father O'Flynn, suspecting this might happen, goes into a field, puts on his cassock and waits. Soon, he sees Paddy coming up the road. '*Stop,* Patrick Murphy, are you not ashamed of yourself?'

'Who the hell are you?' asks Paddy.

'I am Jesus Christ,' thunders the priest.

'You're the bugger I'm looking for, then,' replies Paddy. 'Your mother owes me fifty pence.'

* * * * *

Kevin and Paddy, anxious to visit a house of ill repute, were deeply shocked to see a vicar enter the house. 'Did you see that,' said Paddy, 'a vicar paying a visit to those dirty whores? Well, you wouldn't expect anything else from the Church of England.'

A little while later, they saw the local rabbi go inside. 'Well, now I've seen everything. But what would you expect from the Jews?'

Finally, the local priest, Father Murphy, was seen to enter the house. The two men were silent. Then Paddy beamed at his friend: 'Sure, one of them girls was ill and the Father has gone inside to give her the Last Sacraments.'

* * * * *

Quasimodo was in conversation with Dracula: 'You look rough, Drak, what's up?

Drak answers: 'I keep getting these terrible daymares,

they're horrible. I keep waking up in this Catholic house and it's awful.'

'Why is it awful, Drak?' asks Quasimodo sympathetically.

'Because I'm surrounded by bleeding crucifixes.'

*   *   *   *   *

Two Jesuit students were invited to lunch by their parish priest. A large roast chicken was served. At that moment, the priest was called away on urgent parish business. 'Help yourself, don't bother about me,' he said as he left. When he returned an hour later there was nothing left. Later in the afternoon he paid a visit to the farmer. He noticed a chicken in the yard squawking loudly as he was being fed. 'He seems unusually proud,' remarked the priest jokingly.

'He certainly should be,' replied the farmer, 'he has a son in the Jesuits.'

*   *   *   *   *

A Benedictine and a Jesuit agreed that as they both enjoyed smoking, it would be a great help if they were to be allowed to smoke during Meditation. They paid separate visits to Rome to obtain permission.

The Benedictine asked to be allowed to smoke during Meditation. The answer was no.

The Jesuit asked to be allowed to meditate while smoking. The answer was yes.

*   *   *   *   *

A priest was forced to sit next to a Scottish Presbyterian minister in an aeroplane. The stewardess, young and blonde, approached them and offered them a drink. The priest enthusiastically asked for a Scotch, but the minister shook his head with a disgusted look. 'I'd rather commit adultery,' he said with a sour glance at the priest's whisky.

'Indeed?' said the priest, 'I didn't realise we had a choice.'

* * * * *

The Pope, on hearing that a certain lady in Ireland had produced ten children, despatched a Monsignor to grant her his blessing. When he met the lady, the Monsignor was appalled to learn that she was not a Catholic.

'Do you mean to say,' he thundered, 'that I have come all this way to meet a sex-mad Protestant?'

* * * * *

A young girl from a convent school tells Reverend Mother that when she grows up she intends to be a prostitute. Reverend Mother faints with horror and shock, and has to be revived with smelling salts.

'What was that you said you wanted to be?' she says weakly.

'A prostitute,' replies the girl.

Reverend Mother smiles with relief. 'Ah, God be praised; I thought you said a Protestant!'

* * * * *

'Please Father,' said the youth in the confessional, 'I want to confess to the sin of nail-biting.'

The priest shook his head reassuringly. 'That's not a sin, my son,' he said. 'Don't you know that nail-biting is only a substitute for masturbation?'

The youth was deeply shocked by this. 'But Father,' he said, 'there is no substitute for masturbation.'

Father Fitzpatrick was delving into his patient's soul. 'Tell me, John,' he said, 'do you entertain immoral thoughts about women?'

'Certainly not, Father,' was the reply. 'They entertain me.'

*   *   *   *   *

The priest was hearing confessions and as his memory was slipping a little he used to make a chalk mark on his sleeve as each sin was recited; at the end he would add up the marks and give the appropriate absolution. On this occasion the voice of one of his young parishioners was heard.

'Father,' he said, 'I have committed fornication.'

The priest put a mark on his sleeve.

'I took her into a pub and gave her a drink.'

The priest put another mark on his sleeve.

'I took her into the field, kissed her and told her she was the most beautiful girl I'd ever seen.'

The priest put another mark on his sleeve.

'I laid her down on the grass - and then it happened.'

The priest put another mark on his sleeve.

'Who was this unhappy girl?' he said.

The boy answered: 'She was the vicar's daughter.'

The priest rubbed off all the chalk marks and chuckled: 'Ah well,' he said, 'boys will be boys.'

*   *   *   *   *

A lady undressed at Mass looks silly.
One cannot be devout in deshabilly.

The Confessional

A young priest, newly ordained, was hearing his first confessions, the penitent being a girl who was making some pretty startling revelations. Afterwards, the parish priest took him aside. 'Very good,' he said, 'very good indeed for your first confession, but next time let's have a little more "tut-tut-tut" and not so much of the "phew!"'

* * * * *

A Scotsman living on one of the remoter Western Isles was upbraided for his failure to come to confession on the mainland. 'There's no excuse, Jock,' said the priest, 'you have a good air service now.'

'Ah well, it's this way, Father, travelling by air is too expensive for a venial sin and too dangerous for a mortal one.'

* * * * *

'Father, I was looking into a mirror,' said the girl in the confessional, 'and I decided I was beautiful. Was this a sin?'

The priest shook his head. 'No, my child,' he said, 'it was a mistake.'

* * * * *

Seumas was about to enter the little country church to make his confession when the priest stopped him. 'Would you ever do us a favour, Seumas,' he said, 'the church is full, could you come back tomorrow?' and then added rather flippantly, 'There's nothing urgent, is there? You've not committed a murder since your last confession, have you?'

'Surely not, Father,' said Seumas as he left.

On his way back home, he met his friend, Kevin, who was on his way to the church. 'Go home and come back tomorrow, Kevin,' he said, 'they're only hearing the murderers tonight.'

*   *   *   *   *

'Father,' said the young man, 'is it really a sin to sleep with a girl?'

'Well now, my son,' replied the old priest, 'not exactly, but you young men – you don't sleep!'

*   *   *   *   *

Two small boys making their first confession were hesitating as to which should go in first. The elder plucks up his courage and goes in, to emerge smiling with relief, a few moments later. 'It's all right,' he says to his friend, 'he can't hurt you. He's in a cage.'

*   *   *   *   *

A budding convert was being shown round a Catholic church. 'What's that?' he asked, pointing to the confessional.

'Aahhh,' replied the priest, smiling, 'that's the fire escape.'

*   *   *   *   *

Two young Americans, Chuck and Tommie, decide to share an apartment in New York's 42nd Street. Both are very religious: Chuck is Protestant and Tommie is Catholic. Since they don't like being separated on Sunday mornings, they decide that one of them shall change his religion. Tommie takes Chuck to St Patrick's Cathedral for High Mass and Chuck is deeply impressed by the music, the colour, the incense, the ritual and the vestments.

'While you're here,' says Tommie, 'you gotta do the full bit. You must go to confession.'

'What do I do?' asks Chuck.

'You stand in line with those guys,' says Tommie, 'and when you get into the confessional you tell the priest everything you've done wrong and he'll give you absolution.'

Chuck goes inside. After an hour he still hasn't come out, so Tommie returns to the apartment, saying irritably, 'He must be telling the story of his whole goddam life. He can come home when he's through.'

The rest of Sunday passes and no sign of Chuck. Monday and Tuesday go by and Tommie becomes seriously worried. On Wednesday Chuck suddenly appears in the apartment. 'Where in hell have you been?' shouts Tommie, 'I've been going out of my mind.'

'I couldn't help it,' wailed Chuck, 'I've been in jail.'

'Jail!' shrieks Tommie. 'How in hell could you be in jail? I left you in the confessional at St Patrick's.'

'Yeah,' says Chuck sadly. 'That's how it started. I went inside. I did what you told me. I told the guy everything I did wrong. And he told me to do the stations. So I did. And I got as far as Grand Central before the fuzz picked me up.'

*　　*　　*　　*　　*

A newly-ordained priest is hearing his first confession and a man comes in to confess that he'd stolen a leg of lamb. Uncertain what penance he should give to punish him, the priest consults his parish priest. 'Father,' he says, 'there's a man here who's stolen a leg of lamb. What shall I give him?'

'Not a penny more than five shillings a pound,' was the answer.

*   *   *   *   *

A young girl made her first confession and came out crying into her mother's arms.

'He told me to say as a penance three Hail Marys, but I only know one.'

*   *   *   *   *

'Father, is it a sin to pull a cat's tail off?' asked the little boy at confession.

'Indeed it is, my son,' replied the priest. 'What God hath joined together, let no man pull asunder.'

*   *   *   *   *

Tom had not been to confession for years, and to help him the priest guided him through the tortuous avenue of sins.

'Have you committed murder?'

'At least four times, Father.'

'Have you raped anybody?'

'Several times, Father.'

'Stolen anything?'

'Frequently, Father.'

'Adultery?'

'Indeed, yes.'

'Missed Mass at all?'

'Haven't been for twenty years.'
'Have you ever eaten meat on a Friday?'
Tom was visibly shocked.
'What sorta question is that, Father?' he snapped, 'do you think I'm a heathen or something?'

*   *   *   *   *

A young carpenter confessed that he had stolen some wood from a nearby timber-yard in order to make a sideboard for his wife.
'That's a very serious sin, my son,' said the priest sternly, 'and for your penance I want you to go away and make a novena for me.'
'Certainly, Father, if you provide the wood. And if you like I'll make a coffee-table as well.'

*   *   *   *   *

A tailor confessed that he had stolen a roll of cloth from a van.
'I hope you won't make a habit of it,' said the priest.
'Certainly not,' said the tailor, 'I was going to make two suits from it.'

*   *   *   *   *

'If a Protestant wants advice or aid he has to go to his solicitor: I envy the Catholics with their ever-open confessional – it's so much cheaper!'
– Benjamin Disraeli (1804-81)

*   *   *   *   *

The cherub-faced little boy on his way to church punches every child along the way. Asked why, the child replies, 'I'm on my way to confession and I've nothing to confess.'

It was Grand National Day and I went to confession to a priest friend of mine and, not wanting to be recognised, I altered my voice in the dark confessional. After I'd finished, he said, 'I know it's you, now tell me what won the National? I've been stuck in here all day.'

'Mister What, 100-7, and I backed it,' I told him.

'So did I,' he replied, 'and this is the best confession all afternoon.'

*　　　*　　　*　　　*　　　*

There was a man on the run. He had no particular religious persuasion but he did feel burdened with the guilt of his crime and he decided to cleanse himself of it by confession. He entered an Anglican church and asked the vicar to hear his confession. The vicar said such requests were unusual in modern times but as the man was clearly so distressed, he agreed. They sat down at a bench.

'I've committed a fearful crime.'

'What is it? God will forgive.'

'Murder.'

'Get out of this church at once, you monster, or I'll call the police.'

The man left hurriedly and continued on his way. When he saw a Catholic church he decided to try again. He entered and waited outside the confessional for his turn. Finally, he went into the box.

'I've committed a fearful crime, Father.'

'What crime is that, my son?'

'Murder.'

'And how many times, my son?'

*　　　*　　　*　　　*　　　*

The little boy had been sitting close to the confession box door for a long time before Father Malachy noticed him.

'Have you been eavesdropping on these private and sacred confessions all evening?'

'No, Father, I've only been here since the woman who slept with the sailor came out.'

*   *   *   *   *

A priest was giving a rabbi a lesson in the art of confession. The first woman came in.

'Father, I have committed three terrible sins.'

'For your penance place a pound in the offertory box on your way out.'

Another woman came and she also had three terrible sins to confess and she was given the same penance: one pound in the offertory box on her way out.

'You get the idea? asked the priest. 'Now I have to leave for a moment but you can take over.'

The first penitent to approach the rabbi said, 'Father, I have two terrible sins to confess.'

After a pause the rabbi said, 'Put a pound in the offertory box on your way out and then go out and commit another sin. It's three for the pound.'

*   *   *   *   *

An Italian circus visited an Irish village, and on Saturday night some of the performers went to confession. The priest asked one man what he did for a living, in order to be able to give him better advice.

'I am a tumbler,' replied the Italian.

The priest did not understand this, so he asked the man to give him a brief demonstration at the back of the church, while he put his head out of the confessional and watched.

Two old ladies were sitting at the back of the church.

'Well, well, Bridget,' said one, 'it's glad I am I put me clean underwear on, if Father's giving that for the penance tonight!'

*   *   *   *   *

During the war, with shortages of everything, especially clothes, making life difficult for everybody, a Liverpool docker made his confession:

Docker: Father, I have murdered a Protestant Orangeman.

Priest: Do you have any serious sins to confess?

Docker: I stole a pair of shoes.

Priest: What size?

*   *   *   *   *

'Father, I've committed the sin of adultery,' said the teenage boy.

'Who with?'

'Sorry, Father, I can't be answering that question. It wouldn't be right.'

'Was it Mary Malachy?'

'No, Father, it was not.'

'Was it Brigid O'Shea?'

'No, Father.'

'Well, now, was it Sheila Kinross?'

'No, Father.'

'Well, my son, if you refuse to tell me her name I won't give you absolution. You'd better go away and return next week to complete your confession when you're in a more penitent frame of mind.'

The boy leaves and outside the church he is joined by three friends.

'Did you get absolution?' they ask.

'I did not,' he replies with a happy grin, 'but I've got a week off and three good tips.'

*   *   *   *   *

The priest had great difficulty in getting two persistent sinners from his parish to come to confession. At last he succeeded and they both went to the confessional at the same time on either side of him. During the first man's confession, the priest was called away on urgent parish business and had to leave the box. After a while, the two sinners were getting very worried by this prolonged absence. The first put his head out and whispered to the other in panic, 'Quick, Danny, let's get outa here, he's bloody gone for the police.'

*   *   *   *

A decorator was hired to paint the inside of the confessional box for Father Mason. He went inside the box and got down to work. An old lady entered the confessional and, assuming that the priest was in the box, started her confession. Getting no response she goes out and looks inside. 'Goodness me,' she said in surprise, 'I thought Father Mason was inside here.'

'From what I've heard, luv,' replied the grinning painter, 'it's Perry Mason you need.'

*   *   *   *

'Father, I've stolen a piece of rope.'
'Sure, son, but that's not a serious sin.'
'But it had a pig at the other end.'

*   *   *   *

Did you hear about the man who broke all records for the quickest confessions in the parish? All he did was to poke his head round the confessional door and say, 'everything except murder, Father.'

*   *   *   *

A long queue of schoolboys waited outside the confessional. A small boy rushes to the top, jumping the queue, and pokes his head inside the box. 'Father, if one of them fellers confesses to pinching a school cap, well it's mine.'

*   *   *   *

A Jewish boy was courting a Catholic girl.
She: Sorry I couldn't see you last night, but I had to go to confession.
He: I hope you don't tell the old Father all about the things we get up to on the sofa in the front room when your mum and dad are out at bingo.
She: Sure I do, but don't worry, it's all right. I just drop him a quid for himself and he makes things okay for me.
  The next evening, the Jewish boy arrives at the Catholic Church to see the priest.
Father: Aaaah, my son, I suppose you have come for confession.
He: No, Father, not likely. I've come for commission.

*   *   *   *

'Father, I've committed a lot of terrible sins in the past week,' said the man in the confessional, 'but I can't remember any of them. My memory is going. I can't remember *anything*.'

'I'm sorry to hear that, my son,' said the priest, 'how long have you had this trouble?'

'What trouble?' replied the man.

Monsignor Ronald Knox

Monsignor Ronald Knox (1888-1957) was educated at Eton and Balliol College, Oxford, where he was well known as a witty versifier. He was converted in his thirties while he was a fellow of Trinity, and went on to become a famous Catholic priest. He published a new translation of the Bible, theological works, and six detective stories, and he had a wide reputation as a journalist and broadcaster.

A boy at Ampleforth was asked who were the authors of the four Gospels, and replied, 'Matthew, Mark, Luke and John.' Being then asked who was the real author, he replied, 'Monsignor Ronald Knox.'

*　　　*　　　*　　　*　　　*

Knox hated foreign travel, and would have been perfectly happy to spend his entire life in Oxford. His brief trip to Rhodesia in the 1950s was one of the rare times he left England. He was once asked why he had never visited Rome and made a characteristic reply: 'As I am such a poor sailor I have no desire to visit the engine-room.'

*　　　*　　　*　　　*　　　*

When Knox was being entertained at the Irish Seminary of Maynooth shortly after his conversion to Catholicism, the Seminary displayed true Irish hospitality, and the whiskey flowed like water. Pressed to a second drink, the abstemious Knox protested that he had had enough, but to no avail. His glass was filled, again and again. Finally, he exclaimed, 'Gentlemen, no more please. You must remember I'm only a convert.'

An aggressive old lady once approached Knox. 'In spite of what you people say, I know you get paid in cash for giving absolution after confession.' Knox's face at once became very grave.

'This is a serious matter, madam. Either you have been misinformed, or I've been swindled.'

*　　*　　*　　*　　*

Knox was lunching with some priests when a message came to him that a French sailor was in the church and wished to make his confession. Knox departed immediately. On his return, one of the other priests asked if there was any serious language barrier when dealing with French penitents. 'None at all,' said Knox, 'I don't speak much French but my method is simple. Whenever he pauses, I simply interject, *"Oh, vous avez, avez-vous?"*'

*　　*　　*　　*　　*

When Knox started his mammoth task of translating the Bible he called a meeting of clergy to hear their views. One priest rose and suggested that the Bible should be translated into basic English using the 850 most useful words. Knox replied: 'That is an idea, of course. Personally, however, I feel that in translating the Bible we want at our disposal as large a vocabulary as possible. If you restrict it, then why limit to a thousand words? Surely a hundred words would do, or even less – until you come down to the man who has only one adjective.'

*　　*　　*　　*　　*

Knox was a convert and shortly before he was officially received he was congratulated on having had the courage to leave the Anglican Church: 'Thank you,' he said, 'but the decree nisi has not yet been made absolute.'

In a letter to Laurence Eyres, Knox said, 'One of my first reactions when I was converted was: Now I belong to the same Church as Judas Iscariot.'

*   *   *   *   *

Knox never preached his famous sermons impromptu – they were always written out in advance and read from manuscript. As can be seen from their published texts, they were little gems of wisdom, polished, ironic, and elegant. One day he climbed up to the pulpit, took out the sheets of paper containing his sermon and heard a woman nearby whisper to her neighbour: 'Oh dear, another of those dreaded Pastorals!'

*   *   *   *   *

In a conversation with Malcolm Muggeridge he disclosed 'Hearing nuns' confessions is like being nibbled to death by geese.'

*   *   *   *   *

Speaking as an undergraduate at an Oxford Union debate in 1907 or 1908, he said: 'The honourable gentlemen have turned their backs upon their country and now have the effrontery to say that they have their country behind them . . .'

*   *   *   *   *

Knox objected to the use of the vernacular at baptisms: 'The baby doesn't understand English and the Devil knows Latin.'

*   *   *   *   *

In a letter to Lady Acton, Knox wrote: 'I have a superstition that St Thérèse of Lisieux was asked in Heaven whom she would like to have as translator and she replied, "Ronald Knox – he'll mind my style so terribly and the great thing in religious life is to do something you don't like."'

*   *   *   *   *

Knox declared in a letter to Arnold Lunn: 'I prefer Englishmen to the natives of any other country in the world but that isn't going to do them much good, poor dears, at the Day of Judgement.'

*   *   *   *   *

In a letter to Cardinal Griffin, Knox quoted Dr Johnson's famous rebuke to Lord Chesterfield: 'Is not a patron, my lord, one who looks with unconcern on a man struggling for life in the water and when he has reached ground encumbers him with help?'

*   *   *   *   *

The High Anglican claim that Rome broke from the Church of England at the time of the Reformation, was described by Knox as 'Lambeth Palace blowing away from one of its tiles.'

*   *   *   *   *

'A successful translator must get inside the skin of his author. I am now working on the autobiography of St Thérèse de Lisieux. It is not an easy task for a middle-aged, English, male sinner to get into the skin of a young, French, female saint.'

'God will always answer our prayers, but we must remember that the answer will sometimes be "no".'

*   *   *   *   *

'A good sermon should be like a woman's skirt: short enough to rouse the interest, but long enough to cover the essentials.'

*   *   *   *   *

'The church in Heaven is composed of All Saints; the church on earth is composed of All Sorts.'

*   *   *   *   *

'The best definition of faith, hope and charity that I can give is as follows: if I give a lecture and I'm applauded before I begin, then that's faith, if the applause comes half-way, then that's hope, and if it comes at the end, then that's charity.'

*   *   *   *   *

'In view of the fact that art in Catholic churches is so atrociously bad and that in Protestant ones it is so interestingly good, it is surprising that Catholics should pray with their eyes open and Protestants with their eyes shut.'

*   *   *   *   *

'Catholics are people who agree about Catholicism, and about very little else.'

*   *   *   *   *

'There isn't much simplicity in the New Testament; the word really owes its place in our devotional vocabulary to the *Imitation of Christ*. There you will find some thirty references under "simple" and "simplicity", most of them complimentary. It was St Thérèse de Lisieux, so recent a saint that she isn't even mentioned in the *Catholic Encyclopaedia*, who was the person who really put simplicity on the map.'

*   *   *   *   *

'There once was a man who said "God
Must find it exceedingly odd
If He finds that this tree
Continues to be
When there's no one about in the quad." '

*   *   *   *   *

'Thus suave politeness, tempering bigot zeal,
Corrected "I believe" to "one does feel".'
                          – *Absalom and Abitofhell*

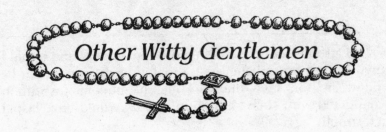

Other Witty Gentlemen

AMBROSE BIERCE (1842–1914)

Christian: One who follows the teachings of Christ insofar as they are not inconsistent with a life of sin.

Heaven: A place where the wicked cease from troubling you with their personal affairs and the good listen with attention while you expound your own.

Saint: A dead sinner, revised and edited.

Sacrament: A solemn religious ceremony to which several degrees of authority and significance are attached. Rome has seven sacraments but the Protestant churches being less prosperous feel they can afford only two, and those being of inferior sanctity – for which mean economy they will indubitably be damned.

Benedictine: An order of monks otherwise known as Black Friars.

Catholic: One who believes that the New Testament is a divinely inspired book admirably suited to the spiritual needs of his neighbours.

Faith: Belief without evidence in what is told by one who speaks without knowledge of things without parallel.

– The Devil's Dictionary

*   *   *   *   *

HILLAIRE BELLOC (1879–1953)

'The Hail Mary was written half by the Church and half by St Gabriel. Dual authorship is seldom a success but the Hail Mary pulled it off all right.'

'The Catholic Church is an institution I am bound to hold divine – but for unbelievers a proof of its divinity might be found in the fact that no merely human institution conducted with such knavish imbecility would have lasted a fortnight.'

On coming down to breakfast one Friday morning in a country house, Belloc asked: 'Are we all Catholics here?' and on receiving an affirmative answer, he said: 'Very well, I shall help myself to a large slice of ham!'

One day he was standing at the back of the church during High Mass. The verger went up to him and said: 'Excuse me, sir, but it's customary to kneel at this point.'

'Oh, go to hell,' snarled Belloc rudely.

The verger retired in confusion. 'I'm very sorry, sir,' he said, 'I didn't realise you were a Catholic.'

*　　　*　　　*　　　*　　　*

VOLTAIRE (1694–1778)

'My prayer to God is a very short one: "Oh Lord, please make my enemies ridiculous." God has granted my wish.'

'When it is a question of money, everybody is the same religion.'

'If God did not exist, it would have been necessary for the Church to have invented him.'

'The history of the Church shows all too clearly that people will kill anybody for the love and greater glory of God.'

'God created woman only to tame men.'

'This agglomeration which was called and which still calls itself the Holy Roman Empire was not holy, nor Roman nor an empire in any way.'

'If God made us in His image, we have certainly returned the compliment.'

*   *   *   *   *

'The fashion now is a Roman Catholic frame of mind with an agnostic conscience: you get the mediaeval picturesqueness of the one with the modern conveniences of the other.'
                                     – Saki (H. H. Munro, 1870–1916)

*   *   *   *   *

'If there was no other proof of the infinite patience of God with men, a very good one could be found in His toleration of the pictures that are painted of Him.'
                                          – Thomas Merton (1915–68)

*   *   *   *   *

'The Church has always been willing to swap treasures in heaven for cash down.'
                                        – R. G. Ingersoll (1833–1899)

*   *   *   *   *

'A little skill in antiquity inclines a man to Popery.'
                                     – Thomas Fuller (1608–1661)

*   *   *   *   *

'The Church thoroughly understands what no other church has ever understood – how to deal with enthusiasts.'
– Lord Macaulay (1800–1859)

*   *   *   *   *

'Here is everything which can lay hold of the eye, ear and imagination – everything which can charm and bewitch the simple and ignorant. I wonder how Luther ever broke the spell.'

– John Adams (1735–1826)

*   *   *   *   *

There was once a priest who used to bore and irritate his brother clergy in the parish by boasting that he could preach a sermon on any subject at a second's notice, be it dull, ordinary or unusual. Eventually they said to him, 'Now put up or shut up. We will write the subject for a sermon on a piece of paper and give it to you as you go to the pulpit and you will either preach the sermon or stop bragging.' 'Accepted,' he said eagerly. The next day a piece of paper was handed to him as he climbed into the pulpit and on it was written one word, '*constipation*'.

'Dearly beloved brethren,' he said as he faced the congregation, 'my mind goes back some 3,000 years when Moses was given two tablets by the Lord and came running down the mountain . . . !'

*   *   *   *   *

'Too hot to go to church? What about Hell?'
– Poster in Dayton, Ohio, USA

*   *   *   *   *

'Bear the Cross cheerfully and it will bear you.'
— Thomas a Kempis (1380–1471)

*　　*　　*　　*　　*

'The only excuse for God is that he doesn't exist.'
— Stendhal (1783–1842)

*　　*　　*　　*　　*

'For 2,000 years the Church has been telling us that life is death and death is life. It's high time to consult a dictionary.'
— Remy de Gourmont (1858–1915)

*　　*　　*　　*　　*

'"One loving soul," says St Augustine, "sets another soul on fire." Evidently the Faith can sometimes be caught as well as taught.'
— Arnold Lunn (1888–1974)

*　　*　　*　　*　　*

'He cannot have God for his father who refuses to have the Church for his mother.'
— St Augustine (354–430)

*　　*　　*　　*　　*

'Kill them all. God will know his own.'
— Arnold of Citeau, Papal Legate
at the seige of Beziers, 1209

*　　*　　*　　*　　*

'This is what the Church is said to want, not party men, but sensible, temperate, sober, well-judging persons to guide it through the channel of non-meaning between the Scylla of Aye and the Charybdis of No.'
– Cardinal Newman (1801–1890)

* * * * *

'Religion is all very well as long as it doesn't interfere with your private life.'
– Lord Melbourne (1779–1848)

* * * * *

'Peter remained on friendly terms with Christ even though Christ had healed his mother-in-law.'
– Samuel Butler (1835–1902)

* * * * *

'The Bible says that the last thing which God made was a woman – it must have been on a Saturday night when He was tired.'
– Alexander Dumas *fils* (1824–1895)

* * * * *

'His was the sort of career which would make the recording Angel think seriously about taking up shorthand.'
– Sydney Smith (1771–1845)

Nuns and Monks

There are a number of marked differences between the Holy Orders which lead to a certain amount of friendly (and not so friendly) rivalry. The Jesuits are primarily a teaching Order and have founded a number of schools of which the best known in England is Stonyhurst; they are zealous in getting converts and are known to have a persuasive way with parents. The Franciscans are famous for their vows of poverty and the devout, mystic simplicity of their lives, whilst the Benedictines are well known for their generous hospitality to strangers.

A Jesuit, a Franciscan and a Benedictine were walking down the road together when they suddenly saw the Holy Family approaching – Joseph leading the donkey, Mary sitting on it holding the Infant Jesus in her arms. All three priests reacted in a highly typical manner: the Franciscan fell to his knees and started to pray, the Benedictine made a mental note that there would be three more for dinner, while the Jesuit rushed forward, shook Joseph warmly by the hand and said:

'He's a splendid little chap, absolutely splendid. And no doubt you'll be sending him to Stonyhurst!'

*   *   *   *   *

The five persons never seen in a monastery are:
1. A learned Carmelite.
2. A poor Benedictine.
3. A clean Franciscan.
4. A truthful Jesuit.
5. A humble Dominican.

A Franciscan, whose order is dedicated to poverty, and a Dominican, whose order is not, were travelling in the country when they suddenly came to a stream with no bridge. The Franciscan was barefoot and his habit was already torn and stained, so the Dominican asked to be carried over.

Halfway across the stream the Franciscan asked the Dominican how much money he had on him.

'Only five pounds.'

The Franciscan promptly dropped his passenger into the water. 'You know the rules. We are not allowed to carry money.'

*   *   *   *   *

A newly-ordained Franciscan priest was invited to meet his bishop, famous for his generous hospitality.

'Will you have a glass of whisky?'

'No thanks.'

'A cup of tea? Or perhaps you'd prefer coffee?'

'No thanks.'

'How about a cigarette – or maybe a cigar?'

'I don't smoke.'

There was a pause and then the rather perplexed bishop asked, 'Well, Father, will you have a Holy Picture?'

*   *   *   *   *

Two Benedictines were deep in conversation. Said the first: 'Well, I'll give it to the Jesuits, they are fine casuists, splendid debaters and marvellous theologians and the Dominicans are superb intellectuals.' The second nodded. 'Quite right,' he said, 'and when it comes to humility, there's not a shadow of doubt that we Benedictines reign supreme.'

There are four things which even God doesn't know:
  1. How much money a Benedictine has.
  2. What a Jesuit is thinking.
  3. What a Dominican is going to say next.
  4. How many Orders of nuns exist in France.

*   *   *   *   *

A novice entered the convent of an enclosed order and on her first day the Mother Superior explained the rules to her.

'The most important is that of total silence. You must not say a word to anybody under any circumstances whatever, but once a year you will come to me and you will be allowed to say one sentence.'

At the end of the first year, the novice was summoned to the Mother Superior's cell.

'You may say one sentence, my child. What is it?'

The novice replied: 'Please, the cell is too cold, I can't sleep.'

The Mother Superior nodded and dismissed her. At the end of the second year, the novice was summoned to the Mother Superior's cell and was allowed to say her second sentence: 'Please, there's never enough food, I'm always hungry.'

Once again she was dismissed without a word.

At the end of the third year, the novice said: 'Please, I'm not happy here, I'd like to go home.'

The Mother Superior frowned angrily. 'I should think so too,' she said, 'you've done nothing but complain ever since you came!'

*   *   *   *   *

A Catholic journalist interviewed the Mother Superior of an Italian convent and questioned her about her wartime experiences.

'The fascists were beasts, my son,' she said. 'You won't believe it, but they broke into the convent and raped every nun, except Sister Mary Anita. Not that the Germans were any better, same story, every nun was raped, except Sister Mary Anita . . . and the Americans; disgusting brutes they were, every nun was raped – except Sister Mary Anita!'

'What's the matter with Sister Mary Anita?' asked the journalist in surprise.

'Aaah, my son,' said the Mother Superior, 'she's not keen on that sort of thing!'

* * * * *

A nun went to Reverend Mother and confessed that she was pregnant.

'Go to the kitchen,' she was told, 'and drink a bottle of vinegar and the juice of five lemons.'

The nun looked surprised. 'But that won't get rid of the baby,' she objected.

'It won't,' agreed Reverend Mother grimly, 'but at least it'll take that smug smile off your face.'

* * * * *

A Jesuit and a Benedictine were discussing their respective housekeepers.

'Mine takes her recipes from the Old Testament,' said the Benedictine sadly.

'What do you mean?' asked the Jesuit.

The Benedictine replied: 'They're either burnt offerings or bloody sacrifices.'

* * * * *

A Jesuit and a Benedictine were discussing their respective clothes.

'God bequeathed us a comfortable habit of ample size,' said the Benedictine, 'whereas you wear a tightly-fitting garment with those ridiculous wings at the back.'

The Jesuit said: 'Surely it's better to have wings than loose habits.'

*   *   *   *   *

There was a gathering of delegates of the different religious Orders. Each member was invited to bring a bottle of something produced by his Order. The Benedictine naturally brought a bottle of Benedictine. The Carthusian brought a bottle of Chartreuse; the Jesuit brought a bottle of disinfectant.

*   *   *   *   *

Ever hear of the nun who had a wooden leg? She was known to the parish as Hopalong Chastity.

*   *   *   *   *

A nun was helped across a busy street by a very small Wolf Cub.

'Thank you very much,' she said, 'you're a very good little boy.'

'That's all right, Sister,' he replied with a grin, 'any friend of Batman is a friend of mine.'

*   *   *   *   *

Two Trappist monks are fishing. One of them catches a very beautiful mermaid, looks at her and then throws her back into the water. The other is so astonished that he momentarily breaks the strict rule of silence by shouting. 'Why?'

The other shrugs his shoulders in frustration and despair and says: '*How?*'

* * * * *

A Dominican, a Benedictine and a Jesuit priest who met in a church began to discuss the relative merits of their Orders. The discussion soon developed into an argument as to which of their three Orders should be considered the senior in terms of importance.

'Surely *we* should be regarded as senior,' said the Dominican, 'since we were created as a direct result of the Albigensian heresy, with a mission to go out into the world and teach the official doctrine of the Church.'

'I cannot agree to that,' said the Benedictine, 'quite obviously we should take precedence as we were created in the sixth century and are the older Order, having steadfastly guarded the liturgy throughout the ages. Anyway, there are about 12,000 of us as compared to only 10,000 of you.'

At last the Jesuit spoke. 'I would be the last to argue our importance on mere numerical strength alone,' he said, 'although there are 36,000 of us active at the moment. However, do not forget that the great burden of the Counter-Reformation in the sixteenth and seventeenth centuries fell on our shoulders, many of our number had to undergo great privations and hardships for the Faith – in fact, we still get the most difficult missionary jobs. Anyway, the Pope's Confessor is always a Jesuit – so we must be the senior.'

By this time the discussion had degenerated into a heated argument and to resolve their dilemma they decided to seek spiritual guidance. The question was duly written on a piece of paper and deposited inside a chalice, which was then placed on the High Altar. After some moments, the chalice rose of its own apparent accord, flew round the church three times and eventually came to rest once more. Peering inside the chalice, the three priests read the following message inscribed on the back of their question paper.

'I wish this unseemly wrangling in my house to cease.'

(signed) GOD, SJ

*   *   *   *   *

Four American priests had been ordained together and agreed to have dinner in a group on the evening of their fifth anniversary. Later they discussed the joys and problems of priesthood.

The first priest said: 'My great problem is gambling. I love it. I know it is wrong and when the urge becomes too great I go to Pittsburgh, check into a hotel, change into civvies and go to a poker club. I lose all my money and come home refreshed with the urge purged out of my system – until the next time.'

The second priest said: 'With me it's drink. Once in a while, I just have to get absolutely blind drunk, so I go to Albany, check into a hotel, put on a robe and the bell-captain brings up a gallon of the stuff. I drink every drop, get deathly sick, stay in the room with a jumbo-sized hangover and then go home sobered up until the urge hits me again, several months later.'

The third priest said: 'With me it's women. I can go for six months without giving sex a thought and then suddenly I've got to have it and right then, so I go to Baltimore, check into a hotel and the bell-captain brings me up a woman, I spend the weekend with her and then I'm okay for another six months.'

The three commiserate with each other and then turn to the fourth and look expectantly at him.

'We told you our problems, Hank,' they said, 'don't you have one of your own?'

'Yeah,' admitted Hank, avoiding their eyes, 'yeah, I guess I do.'

'Well, what is it?'

'I'm a terrible gossip,' said Hank, 'and I just can't wait to get outa here!'

*　　*　　*　　*　　*

Some monks were having a fish and chip dinner. During the festivities one of the guests went to the kitchen and asked, 'Are you the fish frier?'

'No,' was the reply, 'I'm the chip monk.'

*　　*　　*　　*　　*

A woman staggers out of a Dublin bar straight into the arms of a nun. 'Drunk, is it?' said the nun. 'When are you going to learn what evils drink causes?'

'Sister,' asks the woman, 'what is it then that causes dreadful rheumatism?'

'I'll tell you what it is,' snapped the nun angrily, warming to the task, 'it's drinking gin and tonic and smoking and associating with bad men and filling in the football pools. How long have you had rheumatism?'

'Oh, it's not myself that suffers from rheumatism,' said the woman, it's your Mother Superior.'

*　　*　　*　　*　　*

A nun was seen to be running out of a doctor's surgery screaming hysterically.

'What was all that about?' enquired one of the patients in the waiting-room.

'I told her she was pregnant,' said the doctor casually.

'Poor thing, no wonder she was so upset.'

'It isn't true, though.'

'No?'

'No,' replied the doctor calmly. 'But it sure as hell cured her hiccups.'

Miscellaneous

The captain of Beaumont, a famous Jesuit school in Berkshire, sent an invitation to the captain of Eton, suggesting that their respective teams should play a game of cricket. A very insolent letter came back from Eton's captain.

'We have heard of Harrow, we have heard of Rugby, we have heard of Winchester, but we have not heard of you.'

The famous and oft-quoted reply from Beaumont's captain ran as follows: 'Beaumont is what Eton was – a school for the sons of Catholic gentlemen!'

*　　　*　　　*　　　*　　　*

The boys were asked to draw a picture of the flight of the Holy Family out of Egypt for their Religious Instruction class. All but one drew the conventional picture of the rocky mountain pass at night with Joseph leading the donkey and Mary sitting on it holding the Infant Jesus. The exception was a small boy who had taken the word 'flight' quite literally – his picture showed a modern jet-plane flying over the Pyramids. Visible in the plane were four figures, three at the back with a halo, one in the front without a halo.

'Very good,' said the priest-in-charge, 'but who's the man in the front without the halo?'

'Please sir,' said the boy, 'that's Pontius, the pilot.'

*　　　*　　　*　　　*　　　*

It is a strange irony that when the Pope has made a definite ruling against the use of the Pill and other forms of birth control, the name of the leading Catholic newspaper should be *The Tablet*.

*　　　*　　　*　　　*　　　*

'Father, the church is on fire!'
'Holy smoke!'

*　　　*　　　*　　　*　　　*

A young man with a pronounced stutter goes to a dance, sees a pretty girl and asks her to dance with him.
'C-C-C-Certainly I'd l-l-l-l-l-l-love to d-d-d-dance with you,' she says, for she also has a stutter.
Later he says to her, 'B-B-B-By the way, m-m-m-m-my n-n-n-name is P-P-P-P-Peter, but I'm not a s-s-s-s-saint.'
'That's all right,' said the girl, 'M-M-M-M-My name is M-M-M-M-Mary, but I'm not a v-v-v-v-very good dancer.'

*　　　*　　　*　　　*　　　*

Paddy O'Riley had worked long hours in the priest's garden. To reward him the priest invited him in for a drink. 'I'm going to give you something rather special,' he said, 'it is a glass of Benedictine made by the monks at Monte Cassino.'
To Paddy's disappointment the priest poured him out a measure in a very small liqueur glass.
'How did you like it?' asked the priest after Paddy had drained it to the last drop.
'Sure, Father,' was the reply, 'it was God himself who made the drink, but I'm thinking it was the Devil who made the glass.'

At a Deanery conference on a biblical subject, the question was asked, 'Why did the Levite pass by on the other side?' One rather overworked parish priest replied: 'Because he was late and was supposed to be giving confession to some nuns.'

*   *   *   *   *

In the 1920s, the extreme Anglo-Catholic body at Cambridge, which included Wilfrid Knox and Milner-White (afterwards Dean of York), used to refer to Roman Catholics in England as *The Italian Mission.*

*   *   *   *   *

Paddy and Mary and their four children were walking home from Mass after hearing a sermon in which the priest had been stressing the sinfulness of the Pill and the importance of proper and continued sexual relations.

'Paddy,' said Mary, 'do we have any sexual relations?'

Paddy smiled happily. 'Sure we do,' he said, 'why do you ask?'

'Well,' said Mary, 'it's funny that we never hear from them, not even a card at Christmas.'

*   *   *   *   *

During the troubles in Dublin, a scared old Irishwoman was challenged by a sentry. 'Halt, who goes there?' he roared.

'Oh Jesus, Mary and Joseph,' wailed the frightened old lady.

'Pass, Holy Family.'

*   *   *   *   *

On one occasion a full General came down from the War Office to inspect Ampleforth's Junior Training Corps. Being unaware that these were Catholic boys, he addressed them at the end with the statement: 'I feel privileged to speak to a group of boys among whom I feel there might well be numbered not only future Field Marshals, Admirals and Captains of Industry, but possibly even a future Archbishop of Canterbury!'

* * * * *

A monk wearing a habit and a Scotsman wearing a kilt were walking down the street together and the monk was heard to say, 'Well, as a matter of fact, neither do we.'

* * * * *

A priest once observed that an old man who had always, as is the Catholic habit, bowed down his head at the name of Jesus, had now taken to bowing his head at the name of the Devil. When the priest asked him why, he replied, 'Well, Father, politeness costs nothing, and you never know!'

* * * * *

After a Palm Sunday liturgy in St Chad's in 1961, one of the priests who had taken part confessed over lunch that he had suffered during the ceremony from an ungetattable itch. To this Archbishop Grimshaw replied in a flash: 'In the race for perfection, Father, you prefer to start from scratch!'

* * * * *

The American cardinal was at work in his suite of offices overlooking Wall Street when he heard a terrible commotion outside in the street. The centre of interest was a bearded man in long white clothes riding a donkey. The crowd was on its knees, praying, weeping, singing, casting palm-leaves in the donkey's path; the police sirens were topping everything as the riot squads tried in vain to keep control of the situation. The cardinal turned pale and put through a call on the hot line to Rome. 'Holy Father,' he stammered when he finally got through to the Pope, 'Jesus Christ is here riding in triumph through New York! What shall I do?'

The Pope replied irritably, 'Look busy!'

*   *   *   *   *

Oscar Wilde (on his death-bed): Last night I dreamed that I was dining with the damned souls in hell.
Reggie Turner: I've no doubt that you were the life and soul of the party.

*   *   *   *   *

Father Hayes once addressed a meeting of Catholic and Protestant farmers. 'Free speech is welcome on this occasion,' he said. 'Anybody is welcome to say to hell with the Pope, but he must be prepared to prove that hell is a good place for him.'

*   *   *   *   *

A parish priest once bought a cheap pocket watch which continually broke down. Again and again he was forced to take it back to the shop for repairs which became increasingly expensive. When the watchmaker told him finally that the repairs would now cost twice as much as the watch itself, the priest decided to buy a new one. 'I have built up a lot of faith in my old watch,' he said sadly, 'but what is faith without good works?'

* * * * *

A Catholic book-lover in Texas wanted to buy two rare books, *Seekers after God* by Canon Farrar, and *Confidence in God* by Cardinal Newman. He wrote to a New York bookshop for copies and received the following telegram.

'THERE ARE NO SEEKERS AFTER GOD IN NEW YORK STOP NEWMAN'S CONFIDENCE IN GOD ALL GONE.'

* * * * *

The motorist was speeding along happily; his engine was running sweetly and he had a St Christopher medal on his dashboard. Thirty mph . . . forty . . . fifty . . . seventy . . . eighty . . . as the needle trembled over the ninety mph a voice sounded in his ear.

'This is St Christopher speaking. You are on your own now. Over.'

* * * * *

ECUMENICAL CHURCH PARADE

Methodist in Mini
Baptist in his Ford.
Quaker in his Daimler
(Virtue's just reward)
Anglican in Austin
Or Jaguar for choice
And teeming hordes of Catholics
On foot – or by Rolls-Royce.

A schoolboy had saved up for a new bicycle for years, but the first day he rode it, it was stolen. His priest told him to say prayers to St Anthony, which he did. Next day the police rang his home to say the bicycle had been recovered. Overjoyed, the boy collected it and on his way home passed the church. He went inside to say a prayer of thanks to St Anthony but when he came out again, the bicycle had gone.

*   *   *   *   *

The wartime cardinal, the late Cardinal Hinsley was touring round the Irish countryside. In a remote district, a local farmer pointed out such local sights as the Devil's Lake, the Devil's Mountain, the Devil's Marsh, the Devil's Elbow and the Devil's Forest. 'The Devil seems to own a lot of property round here,' commented the Cardinal smilingly.

The farmer scowled resentfully at him. 'Sure that's right, sir,' he said, 'and like most landlords, he spends all of his time in London.'

*   *   *   *   *

An old man, almost blind, shuffled along the street making for the supermarket. Thinking he was entering the shop, he turned into the Catholic Church where the priest, in his High Mass vestments, was walking down the aisle, swinging the thurible. The man peered anxiously at the priest and then rushed forward. 'Please, madam,' he said, 'your handbag is on fire.'

*   *   *   *   *

On the appointment of bishops, the late Cardinal Vaughan once remarked: 'The Spirit breathes where he will, but some people are better than others at getting in the draught.'

*   *   *   *   *

The late Archbishop of Tuam was in the habit, whenever he married a couple, of giving the bride a hearty avuncular kiss after the register had been signed. He was about to do so on one occasion, when the bridegroom tapped him on the shoulder.

'Pardon me, Your Grace,' he said, '*Meam*, not *tuam*.'

*   *   *   *   *

Paddy, on his death-bed, had £50 saved up. The priest and the doctor both visited him: the doctor took £25 to pay for the medical bills and the priest took the other £25 to pay for masses for his soul.

'Will you write a letter to my mother?' asked Paddy. 'Will you write and tell her that I'm dying like Our Blessed Lord did, between two thieves?'

*   *   *   *   *

In the days when Mass was said in Latin, two priests decided to stage a small race to see who could say the Mass quicker. The Jesuit, hearing his rival going straight into the 'Confiteor' and not realising that he was a Dominican and thus using their own version of the Mass, said petulantly, 'Oh well, if you're going to cheat, here goes . . . *Sanctus, Sanctus, Sanctus. . .!*'

*   *   *   *   *

Old lady to priest on January the First: 'Happy Circumcision, father.'

*　　　*　　　*　　　*　　　*

The Welsh claim that they invested St Patrick in the Bank of Ireland more than 1,500 years ago and are now drawing the interest in priests serving in Wales.

*　　　*　　　*　　　*　　　*

Cardinal Hinsley was once called on to give evidence in a court case, and to impress the jury, the defence counsel asked if he was the leader of the English Catholics.

'That's right,' said the Cardinal.

'In fact, you are the Prince of the Church in Rome?'

'Correct.'

'One of the greatest scholars not only in England but in the whole world?'

'True.'

'A brilliant man in every way?'

'Yes.'

Later, a friend reproached the Cardinal. 'You weren't very humble today, were you?'

The Cardinal smiled. 'True,' he said, 'but what could I do? I was on oath.'

*　　　*　　　*　　　*　　　*

In the early days of international aviation, a plane circling over Shannon Airport in Ireland radioed to the control tower that its engines were on fire.

'What shall I do?' asked the pilot in a panic.

The voice from control said:

'Repeat after me the Act of Contrition: Oh my God, I am sorry for my sins. . .'

Most people know the religious as well as the sporting rivalries which enliven the games between the two famous Glasgow football teams – the Catholic Celtics and the Protestant Rangers. During one Cup Final at Ibrox Park the Celtic side was losing, largely due to lethargic playing from the forwards.

'Play up the forwards,' shouted one Celtic supporter.

'They're not forwards,' commented his mate, 'they're the Five Sorrowful Mysteries.'

*   *   *   *   *

Dennis, a Catholic boy, and Jock, a Protestant boy, were great friends, even though Dennis supported Celtic and Jock the Rangers at the weekly football match in Ibrox Park. Tired of religious bigotry, they decided to visit each other's churches one Sunday. Dennis went with Jock to the Kirk and Jock went with Dennis to High Mass. Jock was noticeably fuming as he came out.

'What's troubling you?' asked Dennis.

'It's bad enough when he wears Celtic colours,' complained Jock, 'but it was worse when he started to wave the European Cup about.'

*   *   *   *   *

'Can you hear what they're saying?' said one small boy to another who was listening through the door of a Catholic church.

'Yes,' said the other, 'they're saying: "Dominick, is the biscuit come?" and the other bloke's saying, "Yes, and the spirits too!"'

*   *   *   *   *

111

Small boy reciting the Confiteor:
>   To Blessed Mary never a virgin
>   To Blessed Michael Angelo
>   To Blessed John, the tobacconist
>   To the Holy Apostles, sweet and tall. . .

*   *   *   *   *

Small boy reciting The Lord's Prayer:
> Our Father who shouts in heaven, Harold be Thy name, blessed art thou a monk swimming. . .

*   *   *   *   *

Heard during the Divine praises: 'Blessed be St Joseph and his jazz blouse. . .'

*   *   *   *   *

Heard during the Apostle's Creed: '. . .crucified under a bunch of violets. . .'

*   *   *   *   *

A little boy was listening to a long and excessively boring sermon in church. Suddenly his eye was caught by the red votive lamp by the sanctuary. Tugging his father's sleeve he said: 'Father, when it turns green, can we go?'

*   *   *   *   *

A visiting bishop in a small country parish was introduced to a good local Catholic mother who had ten children, all boys. 'Was it a boy every time?', he asked.

'Ah no, my Lord,' she replied, 'several times it was nothing at all.'

*   *   *   *   *

Paddy is standing in the middle of the road and a huge Rolls-Royce passes him and just touches him. Knowing what to do, Paddy falls down on the ground, writhes in a convincing display of agony and shouts, 'Ah, me back, me back, me back!' and he won't move until the ambulance arrives and takes him to hospital. After three weeks of examination and treatment the doctors can't find anything wrong with him; all Paddy has to do is scream, 'Aaaah, me back, me back!' when anybody so much as touches him.

Eventually a court case is brought and the judge awards him heavy damages. 'Thank you, y'honner,' moans Paddy as he is wheeled out of the court.

An insurance man follows him and succeeds in having a few quiet words with him in the ambulance. 'You might have fooled the doctors and the judge,' he says sternly, 'but you can't fool me. If you so much as take a step out of that chair I shall know about it, because I'm going to follow you around for the rest of your life and then you'll lose your sixty thousand pounds and you'll go to prison.'

'Is that a fact?' says Paddy, 'well, I hope you're a Catholic like me.'

'What's that got to do with it?' asks the insurance man.

'Just this,' says Paddy. 'I'm going straight to Dublin Airport now and from there to Lourdes and if you are right behind me like you say, you'll then see the fastest miracle you've ever seen in your life.'

*   *   *   *   *

One of the popular cabaret jokes in Hitler's Germany was about Goering who was well known for his love of dressing-up.

One day Hitler demanded that the Pope should give his public approval and endorsement of Nazism. The Pope naturally refused so Goering was sent to teach him a lesson. All was silence for a fortnight, then a telegram arrived at Berchtesgarten.

'POPE DEAD. ROME BURNS. PATERNAL BLESSINGS. YOUR HOLY FATHER HERMANN.'

*　　*　　*　　*　　*

The late Cardinal Vaughan was once criticised by a non-smoker for enjoying his pipe. The Cardinal replied: 'I would much rather smoke in this world than in the next.'

*　　*　　*　　*　　*

Cardinal Vaughan was once a guest at an unspeakably dreary dinner organized in his honour by some northern civic dignitary, but he succeeded in enlivening it by his speech of thanks.

'Ladies and Gentlemen,' he said, 'there is an old tradition in the Catholic Church that when a baby is born it is kissed by its Guardian Angel for luck. If the baby is kissed on the head, it becomes very brainy, if on the hands it becomes a clever craftsman or musician, if on the lips then a great singer or conversationalist. Now, I don't know where my host, His Worship the Lord Mayor, was kissed, but he certainly makes a very good Chairman.'

*　　*　　*　　*　　*

114

In my day, men were content with ten commandments and
one wife. Now the situation is reversed.

– Saki (H.H. Munro, 1870–1916)

* * * * *

Surgeon Oliver Gogarty was performing a difficult opera-
tion. Suddenly, the theatre sister said: 'May Jesus, Mary
and Joseph help us,' to which he replied: 'Thank you,
sister, but I don't want any unqualified assistance.'

* * * * *

The penny and the pound had become close friends before
they left the Royal Mint. Five years later they met in a
tobacconist's till. What a tale the pound had to tell – trips
to the continent, night-clubs, gambling casinos, theatres
and expensive restaurants.

'Well,' said the penny, 'I've spent most of my life in and
out of slot machines but I can truthfully say one thing for
myself – I never once missed Mass on a Sunday.'

* * * * *

Sign in a Catholic butcher's shop: This bacon was cured in
Lourdes.

* * * * *

Adam and Eve are in the Garden of Eden:

Eve: Do you love me, honey?
Adam: Who else?

* * * * *

The priest in charge of a Catholic church in Ireland decided to install a public address system so that his sermon from the pulpit could be heard by the latecomers at the back of his church.

When the installation had been completed the priest thought it would be a good idea to test it out. So he went into the pulpit and saw what seemed fortunate at the time, an elderly lady on her knees in the front row saying her rosary more or less aloud. With the volume at its lowest he took the mike, saying, 'You are listening to the word of Jesus.'

Looking down at the lady saying her rosary, he was surprised that she had not taken the slightest notice. He decided to repeat the words with the volume turned halfway up; still she just went on audibly with her Hail Marys. In sheer desperation he turned the volume to its fullest, again repeating, 'You are listening to the word of Jesus.'

The elderly lady at last looked up. 'Would you mind keeping quiet while I'm talking to your mother?'

*   *   *   *   *

The basic problem with the Catholic church in America is that it has too many Catholics and not enough Christians.

*   *   *   *   *

It was the Emperor Diocletian's birthday. One little Early Christian Martyr was heard to mutter to himself from up on his cross. The Emperor tried hard to hear but couldn't.

'What are you muttering?' he asked.

The little Early Christian continued to mutter inaudibly.

Finally, the Emperor told one of the guards to climb up and listen. He did so: 'He is saying "Happy birthday to you,"' he reported.

116

Three Early Christian Martyrs, having been nailed to the cross, were burned. The soldier lighting the fire round the first and second paused before the third and looks up hopefully at the Christian, saying, 'I hope you're not superstitious.'

*   *   *   *   *

A Catholic bishop, in passing a group of little boys, placed his loving hand on the head of one of them and said, 'God bless you.'

The little boy looked up. 'Who sneezed?' he asked.

*   *   *   *   *

'. . .G.K. Chesterton was right when he said that the failure of Christianity was due to the fact that it had never been tried. There would never have been such a thing as communism if Christians had even tried to live as Christians. . .'

– *The Bishop*, Bruce Marshall

*   *   *   *   *

Archbishop Heenan was touring Ireland and he chanced to visit a little church in a remote parish. He announced to the parish priest his intention of saying High Mass on the following day and preaching a sermon, and so he did – but only a few people turned up to hear him.

'It's not a good turn-out,' he complained to the priest. 'Didn't you tell your parish that I would be preaching?'

'That I did not, Your Eminence,' said the priest, 'but I'll find out who did.'

*   *   *   *   *

A loud-mouthed, boastful man was holding forth very boringly at a luncheon given by the Legion of Mary. 'I've always made a point of going to Lourdes every year.'

A foolish young girl smiled at him. 'That's funny,' she giggled, 'you don't look a bit like a man who's interested in cricket.'

*   *   *   *   *

Three men in a Dublin pub were trying to outboast each other.

'I was once mistaken for Winston Churchill,' said the Englishman.

'I was once mistaken for General de Gaulle,' said the Frenchman.

'I once went to a cinema where they had a continuous showing day and night,' said the Irishman. 'I sat through the first programme, and the second and then the third, and in the middle of the fourth showing the attendant approached me and said, "Jesus Christ, are you still here?"'

*   *   *   *   *

A young Protestant soldier, posted to Italy during the war, found himself in love with two Catholic girls, Rosa and Maria. Which one should he marry? The local priest advised him to go inside the church and pray for guidance. He did so. Later, he rushed out and went to the priest in a state of great excitement. 'It really works, Father, just as you said. I got my answer plain as it could be. I looked up at the altar and there written in large letters of gold were the words, "*Ave Maria*".'

*   *   *   *   *

The priest was calling round at his parishioners' homes, but not on his usual day. He knocked on the door of one of them, a poor man with several children.

'What is the honour of this unusual visit, Father?'

'I'm calling to collect money for a motorbike because I cannot get round my parish on foot.'

'I'm sorry, Father, I have no money.'

'Thanks very much, Pat,' replied the priest, but as he left the house he accidentally knocked over a vase on the sideboard which revealed a pile of banknotes underneath. 'I am disgusted with you, Pat,' he exclaimed.

'But, Father, the money is for a hair perm for the wife.'

'The Virgin Mary never had a hair perm.'

'And Jesus Christ never had a motorbike.'

*   *   *   *   *

Some years ago, when the Mass was still said in Latin, an Irish village had two pubs, and there were three applicants for the licences. Murphy was an evil man, but Christie and Carey were good men. All three went to the parish priest and asked him to pray for them, which he promised to do.

In due course Christie and Carey were appointed licensees, but Murphy was not. The latter, blind drunk, stormed up to the presbytery and started abusing the priest, accusing him of not praying for all three.

The priest defended himself: 'But I did pray for you, my son.'

Murphy retorted: 'No you did not! I went to Mass on Sunday for the first time in forty years. There yer were, standing at the altar. 'Carey a licence' yer said t'ree times, then 'Christie a licence' t'hree times, then 'Carey a licence' t'hree times more, but yer didn't say 'Murphy a licence' even once!'

*   *   *   *   *

It was Cardinal Spellman who forbade the custom of preaching a panegyric at the funeral of a priest, as he didn't like the idea of two priests lying at the same time.

*   *   *   *   *

The teacher was telling her young charges about the beauty and happiness of Heaven. Summing it up, she said, 'Heaven is a place of eternal bliss.'

One of her more precocious pupils immediately added, 'Yes, miss, and Hell is a place of eternal blisters.'

*   *   *   *   *

There was this man who believed in nothing. Hell, Heaven, Purgatory, Limbo – you name it, he didn't believe in it. Finally, death caught up with him and a friend went to the funeral parlour to see him laid out. Later, other friends heard all about it. 'There he was, a lovely dress suit, snow-white ruffled shirt, white tie, the lot. All dressed up and nowhere to go.'

*   *   *   *   *

A priest, who was deeply interested in racing, absent-mindedly told his congregation, 'This is the first Sunday after Pontefract.'

*   *   *   *   *

Mr Jones: How long is it since Father Prendergast left this parish?
Johnny: Thirteen weeks, sir.
Mr Jones: That's a wonderful memory, how can you be so sure?

120

Johnny: Oh, I didn't remember it. But at Mass this morning, Father Murphy said it was the thirteenth week after Prendergast.

*   *   *   *   *

A mugger held up a man in a dark street in Chicago and demanded his wallet. When the man opened his coat, the gangster noticed his clerical collar. 'I'm sorry, Father,' he exclaimed in embarrassment, 'I didn't know that you were a priest. Put your wallet away. I'm sorry.'

The priest took out a dollar and gave it to him. 'There you are, my son, have a dollar at least and God bless you.' The mugger shook his head.

'Well, have a cigarette,' said the priest.

'No thanks, Father, I don't smoke during Lent.'

*   *   *   *   *

Mother: I hope you were a good boy at High Mass this morning?

Son: Yes, mother. A kind gentleman offered me a plate of money but I said 'No thank you.'

*   *   *   *   *

A small girl was travelling with her mother to Windsor. Suddenly she exclaimed in excitement, 'Look, Mummy, is that where God means when he says Lead Us Not Into Thames Station.'

*   *   *   *   *

The three students went as usual to their favourite local restaurant for lunch and made for their usual table by the window, only to discover a Catholic priest occupying one of the seats. They decided that they would sit there all the same and try to embarrass the priest into moving. Thus, seating themselves at the table, they executed their plan of action.

Turning to the other two students, one remarked: 'Did you know that I was born only two months after my parents were married?'

The second said: 'I can beat that; my parents were only married one week before I was born.'

The third announced: 'This very afternoon I intend to write out invitations to my parents' marriage.'

At this, the Catholic priest looked up and said brightly: 'Would one of you bastards care to pass the salt?'

*   *   *   *   *

There was this priest who for some reason was unable to replenish his supply of Holy Water.

'That must indeed be terrible,' commiserated a friend.

'Not at all,' replied the priest, 'I simply put a kettle of ordinary tapwater on the hob and boil the hell out of it.'

*   *   *   *   *

The priest was instructing the class in religious knowledge. 'Like fat and lean in bacon, some of us are good and some are bad. Brigid, if you were bacon, what would you be?'

'Streaky.'

*   *   *   -   *   *

Falkirk

Dear Mr Huggett

I refer to your letter in *The Stage*.

You will find it very difficult to publish a collection of good
Catholic jokes for next Christmas, as there is no such thing
as a good Catholic!

yours sincerely,

(V. Pohler, Miss)

Acknowledgements

I wish to offer my thanks to the following for their permission to quote, which permissions are hereby acknowledged:

Tony Butler and the Wolfe Publishing Company BEST IRISH JOKES, BEST RELIGIOUS JOKES.

A.P. Watt & Son and Lord Oxford, owner of the Ronald Knox estate.

Curtis Brown, PRIVATE LIVES, by Noël Coward.

A.D. Peters, Ltd, and executors for the late Hilaire Belloc.

Harvey Unna, Andre Deutsch and Peter Luke, HADRIAN THE SEVENTH.

Malcolm Muggeridge and the estate of Kenneth Tynan for permission to quote from their writings.

John Osborne for permission to quote from THE ENTERTAINER.

The Harvill Press and Henri Fesquet, THE WIT AND WISDOM OF GOOD POPE JOHN.

The Abbot of Gethsamane, Kentucky, USA, executor of the late Thomas Merton.

John Yates, author of RUGBY JOKES (Sphere Books).

*　　*　　*　　*　　*

I would also like to offer my grateful thanks to the following who have contributed jokes and witticisms, have helped by suggesting fields of research or have rendered valuable assistance in other ways.

Amy Albright, Mary Allen, Mirriam Allen deFord, Miss J. Ausden, Louise Barriere, S.J. Bedwell, M.J. Bejlovec, A. Bell, Angela Bennett, John Benoy, Mrs Brady, Mrs Broadhurst, Hugh Bryan, Kenneth Buckley, Richard Bundy, Joyce Carpenter, A.A. Clifton, Mrs Anne K. Clohesy, Mrs Eileen Collins, Wally Coterave, Nicholas Cowper, John H. Coxall, The Rev. R.L. Crampton, Major Danagher, David Dennison, E. Devine, P.J. Dineen, T. Edward Dixon, T. Stuart Dixon, Miss C. Donnelly, Miss G.E. Doyle, William Drennon, J.A. Duigan, Kathleen E. Dunston, Mrs Veronique Eaton, Fr. P. Fielden, Denham Ford, Patrick Garland, J.C.G. George, Armand Georges, Daniel Gilfeather, Alfred Glenn, William Glennon, Benny Green, C.S. Green, Richard Griffith, J. Hale, Arthur Halliday, Arthur Harvey Wood, The Rev. Jerome Hay, W.O.I.G. Hayden, Mrs. Heady, Dorothy Higgins, Faith Hines, Rolande Hirst, K.J. Hirschfeld, Marjorie Hodge, Mrs Dorothy Holliwell, L.M. Howse, Martin Hutchinson, K.G. Jackson, Miss U.S. Collette Jones, The Rev. E. Keelaghan, Joseph A. Keller, Miles Kington, Unity Kirke, Glenn D. Kittler, Wayne Klatt, Barbara Lambert, John Lane, J.L. Langron, J.B. Lansberry, Malcolm Lawson-Paul, S. Lucia, William Mackey, D.P. MacSheahan, Mrs Winifred Mahony, Mrs Mariey McCarron, Peter McCauley, Peter McClaren, J. McCormick, Cecil McCracken, Thomas McLachlan, James Mellors, Alec Merivale, Richard Miller, George Mills, J. Molloy, The Rev. Montague Cosa, J. Mulholland, Mrs Naylor, A.J. Nazareth, Michael O'Callaghan, D.J. O'Neill, John O'Sullivan, James Oswald, Thomas Paterson, Monica Pearce, Thomas Piney, E.L. Powell, Syd Prin, Miss N. Pryce-Jones, Dr T.G. Reah, C.J. Rice, G.A.L. Rutledge, Richard Savage, Frank Shaw, William Shipp, Barry Sinclair, Bob Smith, Godfrey Smith, Robert Speight, B.G. Spracklin, Leslie Strickland, Leslie Stuart, Malcolm Tudor, John Tynan, Heribert Wagener, Joan Wallace, J.T. Walsh, H.A.H. Walter, Mrs Gwynneth Ward, Fr. Jasper White, Katherine Whitehorn, Joe Wiebkin, H. Wigzell, Mrs Naomi Verne.